PRAISE FOR *THE LEADER-SHIFT PLAYBOOK*

"*The Leader-Shift Playbook* is a powerful and practical guide to unlocking the potential within yourself and your team."

—GINO WICKMAN, best-selling author of *Traction* and *Shine*, creator of EOS®

"For anyone who wants to make a positive impact, *The Leader-Shift Playbook* provides a powerful framework for leading with vulnerability and purpose to create a better business and a better world. Phil Wilson shares his own story of discovering the path of servant leadership. His book will challenge you to embrace your imperfections and connect with your team on a human level."

—HOWARD BEHAR, former president of Starbucks Coffee International, best-selling author of *It's Not About the Coffee*

"If you want to be a cutting-edge leader, you need to read this book. Phil Wilson outlines an essential playbook for anyone in a leadership position."

—VANESSA VAN EDWARDS, best-selling author of *Cues*, founder of Science of People

"A must-read for leaders ready to create a lasting impact. *The Leader-Shift Playbook* offers a masterful guide to shifting mindsets and elevating team performance through simple but profound changes."

—DAVID BURKUS, best-selling author of *Best Team Ever*

"Ready to level up your leadership game? *The Leader-Shift Playbook* is your new go-to guide! Phil Wilson spills the secrets on building teams that actually want to work together, communicate like pros, and feel like they belong. Say goodbye to boring leadership tips and hello to a playbook that'll totally shift how you lead!"

—ERIN DIEHL, keynote speaker, best-selling author of *I See You!*

"This book isn't just about leadership at work—it's about becoming the best version of yourself. Phil's insights in *The Leader-Shift Playbook* offer practical tools to improve your relationships, boost your confidence, and live a more fulfilling life."

—CARRIE RUST, chief HR officer of ELLWOOD Group Inc.

"Phil Wilson does it again! He has followed up *The Approachability Playbook* with another winner, *The Leader-Shift Playbook*. His latest playbook provides easy-to-execute exercises and tools that will improve your leaders' abilities to engage their people, which, in turn, will drive results. I know this to be true because I'm a dispositional optimist!"

—MICHAEL ESPOSITO, president of Espo Employee Relations LLC, former SVP of labor strategy at XPO Logistics

"*The Leader-Shift Playbook* provides a highly accessible and insightful road-map for anyone looking to become a better leader—and have a better life. Using personal anecdotes, research, and self-deprecating humor, Phil Wilson outlines the tools and techniques that anyone, from an experienced Fortune 500 CEO to a newly minted frontline supervisor, can use to achieve their full potential and superior results."

—NICK KALM, founder and CEO of Reputation Partners LLC

"Creating a positive workspace where managers and employees feel valued and heard is like an athletic event. Working with Phil Wilson's philosophies helps managers become more confident, dedicated, and valued, thereby creating a culture that fellow employees absorb. While you can't hit a home run every day in the workplace, Phil's guidance encourages everyone to try."

—DAVID HADDAD, CEO of Haddad's Inc.

"With a heavy dose of humor and humility, Phil takes the reader through his journey as a leader. His story is a powerful example all leaders can learn from, whether you're new to management or you've been at it for thirty years. I highly recommend this book for anyone who leads people and look forward to implementing Phil's four 'simple changes' with my team."

—DAREN WINGARD, vice president of associate relations, C.R. England

THE LEADER-SHIFT

SHIFT

//////IPLAYBOOK(((((((((((((

4 SIMPLE CHANGES TO SCORE BIG

AND UNLEASH YOUR TEAM'S POTENTIAL

THE

LEADER-

SHIFT

//////PLAYBOOK(((((((((((((

PHILLIP B. WILSON

**FAST
COMPANY**
Press

Fast Company Press
New York, New York
www.fastcompanypress.com

This work is being published under the Fast Company Press imprint by an
exclusive arrangement with *Fast Company*. *Fast Company* and the *Fast Company*
logo are registered trademarks of Mansueto Ventures, LLC. The Fast Company
Press logo is a wholly owned trademark of Mansueto Ventures, LLC.

Approachable Leadership is a registered trademark of Labor
Relations Institute, Inc.

Distributed by Greenleaf Book Group

For ordering information or special discounts for bulk purchases, please
contact Greenleaf Book Group at PO Box 91869, Austin, TX 78709,
512.891.6100.

Design and composition by Greenleaf Book Group
Cover design by Greenleaf Book Group

Publisher's Cataloging-in-Publication data is available.

Print ISBN: 978-1-63908-117-2

eBook ISBN: 978-1-63908-118-9

To offset the number of trees consumed in the printing of our books, Greenleaf
donates a portion of the proceeds from each printing to the Arbor Day
Foundation. Greenleaf Book Group has replaced over 50,000 trees since 2007.

Printed in the United States of America on acid-free paper

25 26 27 28 29 30 31 32   10 9 8 7 6 5 4 3 2 1

First Edition

CONTENTS

GREETINGS FROM MOUNT STUPID

*"The thing always happens that you really believe in;
and the belief in a thing makes it happen."*
—Frank Lloyd Wright

October 2019 was when I cracked. Standing in my room at the Santa Monica Courtyard Inn, my world was spiraling out of control. I'd traveled twenty-seven days for work that month, speaking at conferences in San Diego, Las Vegas, and New Orleans. Client emergencies sent me to a major health care client in Cincinnati, a technology company in Los Angeles, and an aerospace organization in Chicago. I managed to keep most of the plates spinning, but I wasn't sure how I was going to keep it up. I needed help.

The only person who knew about my struggle was my close friend Nate. He knew because I'd decided he was the guy who could save me. Nate had just left his accounting firm and was launching, with my encouragement, a business strategy firm. On one of my few days home that month, he and I had lunch. Over a platter of barbecue, I asked if he'd join my company as our chief of staff.

"What does a chief of staff do?" Nate wisely asked. I stammered around, mostly listing a bunch of the spinning plates I thought were about to crash. He replied, "I have no idea whether I can do any of that, but why don't you send me a job description, and I'll take a look." The next day I hopped on a flight and started typing up the job description. Three pages later, my plane landed and I hit Send as soon as I got a Wi-Fi signal.

An hour later (it probably took him that long to read what I'd written), Nate called. "Are you nuts? This is at least three jobs! No wonder you're so overwhelmed. How long have you been trying to do all this?"

"A long time," I sheepishly replied.

Then came the gut punch. "No way I could do this. And I don't think a chief of staff is going to solve your problems." He was too kind to add what he was really thinking: *You need to be a better leader.*

Our employee relations consulting company had been founded forty-five years earlier by my father, and I joined the business in 1997. I took over the day-to-day operations ten years later, and we grew into a multimillion-dollar consulting practice. But by 2019 the company was stuck, and it was all my fault.

Everything funneled through me. And I was so busy working with clients and speaking that I never had any time to work on the business or care for our team. We're a small organization—we were eleven employees in 2019 and only thirteen today as I write this—but even so, we were siloed and flailing.

We'd hit a plateau. We were in our fourth year of no growth. Our culture was flat too. In 2019, if you'd asked anyone on the team about what it was like to work for us, they'd say, "It's like a family." That wouldn't technically be wrong. Several on the team had worked there for more than a decade. But our family put the "fun" in dysfunctional. And that dysfunction started with me.

Ironically, while I was traveling the country speaking and delivering workshops on leadership, my own company was a poster child for bad leadership. We had no common direction—any direction we had was whatever shiny object I'd decided we should chase that month. And most people weren't too excited chasing that shiny object, knowing I'd be chasing a different one the next month. I was doing a terrible job of delegating, and I was a bottleneck.

Even worse, a big reason I was such an obstacle was I just didn't trust my team. I made assumptions about their capabilities and didn't think I could count on them to do the work the way I wanted it done.

Nate continued, "If you look at that job description, one thing is clear. You're the problem here. Everything goes through you. You don't need a chief of staff; you need a system."

I'd always thought of myself as a good leader. Heck, some days I thought I was a great leader. If only I had a little help, then I'd achieve all my lofty goals. Suddenly it was clear I'd completely missed the boat. I felt like a failure and a fraud.

Nate agreed to help me implement a new operating system for

our company. But I would have to promise that this was not just another whim. I'd have to commit to trusting the process and trusting my team. My default assumptions about my team would have to shift, and I would have to trust them to achieve our vision. I would have to change some ingrained habits.

The good news is that I already had ideas on how to do this. I'd been teaching and writing about these same principles for years. And I'd even had success helping other companies overcome similar challenges. Now it was time to start drinking my own champagne.

I needed to change my beliefs about leadership—the beliefs I had about myself and the beliefs I held (pretty much completely erroneous, by the way) about my teammates. All the best practices I knew and all the plans we could design wouldn't change anything unless we changed—unless we adopted a new mindset. It all came down to four fundamental shifts in how we saw ourselves and one another. It became the journey I call the Leader-Shift—and it has nothing to do with ego and grand plans, which you'll understand very soon.

I want to help you do the same thing for yourself, right now. I want to help you tap into your own new mindset and make the four shifts of positive leadership that will make an immediate difference in the culture and lives of your team (and yourself). These shifts will change the way you see and connect with your team and help you contribute to a company culture in which each person feels encouraged and inspired to reach their highest potential. It puts the power back into your hands, even on those days when you feel stalled or uncertain.

WHAT IF I'M A FRONTLINE LEADER?

What if you're not a company owner? You may wonder, *How does this guy's struggles running a company relate to* me *leading a team inside a company?* Great question.

I know a lot about the struggles of frontline leaders. My day job for the last thirty years has been helping leaders just like you. My team and I get up every day to support frontline leaders in both small and large companies, in every industry you can think of, all over the United States and Canada. Whether it's a nursing leader in an acute care setting, a manager of a retail location, a warehouse supervisor, or a department head in a manufacturing facility, we've helped every kind of leader in every kind of environment.

Our firm tends to intersect with leaders in companies that are in crisis. This is when the leadership chips are really down on the table. And for decades we've successfully helped struggling leaders in these tough situations strengthen connections with their teams and turn around their culture.

For most of our company's existence, our work was done one-on-one, coaching frontline leaders and higher-level managers through these tough times. Over the last ten years, we took everything we learned about leadership and began teaching these principles in our Approachable Leadership® Workshops and in our book *The Approachability Playbook.* Thousands of leaders have transformed their relationships with their teams following these principles. Whether you've attended one of our workshops or read *The Approachability Playbook* (if not, I hope you will!), this book will help you further your own personal leadership and your connections with your team.

But my journey of making big shifts over the last four years has taught me that there is a significant difference between knowing *what* to do and actually *doing it*. The other thing I've learned is that the fundamentals of leading a team don't change, whether you are leading a company or a department or even a group of volunteers in your community. That's why I think it's important that you also hear my personal leadership story (in addition to the tools and insights I've used and tested along the way).

My hope is that this story will inspire you to make these same shifts with your own team. As you think about how these lessons apply to your own department, remember that even though my position might be different from yours, my leadership challenges were the same. As the frontline leader for my own team, I am responsible for our day-to-day relationships and culture. My beliefs and assumptions about each member of our crew impact how I behave, speak, and relate to them, which determines whether we'll have a strong connection. These connections alone are the difference between a culture that thrives and performs and one that fails.

So take a moment and ask yourself: How do I think I'm doing as a leader?

Richard P. Feynman once said, "The first principle is that you must not fool yourself, and you are the easiest person to fool." Four years ago, I would have told you I was doing a pretty good job as a leader. But I was actually failing. And that brings us to Mount Stupid.

ARE YOU AS GOOD (OR BAD) A LEADER AS YOU THINK?

"In all affairs, it's a healthy thing now and then to hang a question mark on the things you have long taken for granted."
—BERTRAND RUSSELL

Maybe you're like I was and think you are doing a great job as a leader when you're actually causing a lot of problems. On the other hand, and what is often the case with frontline leaders, you may think you're failing, and with all the pressures you face, you may feel powerless to have the influence and impact you'd like with your team. Regardless of the current state of things, there's a good chance you're not seeing your situation clearly. That's because leadership is *hard*, and you don't just become a great leader because you've been given a title or have seniority or are an expert at the jobs you supervise.

One of my favorite shows is *The Office*, featuring the world's greatest boss Michael Scott (he's got the coffee mug to prove it). On the episode called "Survivor Man,"[1] after being left out of a camping trip, Michael decides to prove his wilderness skills by blindfolding himself and asking his salesman Dwight Schrute to strand him in the woods for a few days.

It quickly becomes clear that not only is Michael Scott not an outdoorsman, but he has drastically underestimated how little he knows about surviving in the wilderness. He ends up comically trying to fashion a shelter out of a cut-up pair of pants. He fights off hunger by grabbing some poisonous wild mushrooms, only to be saved at the last minute by Dwight, who stayed in the woods knowing Michael couldn't survive on his own.

As anyone who has watched the series knows, Michael Scott's overconfidence about his abilities is a recurring theme. It's a great illustration of the Dunning-Kruger effect[2]—the cognitive bias of incompetent people who often overestimate their abilities. Once someone grows in skill and knowledge, they begin to understand what they don't know.

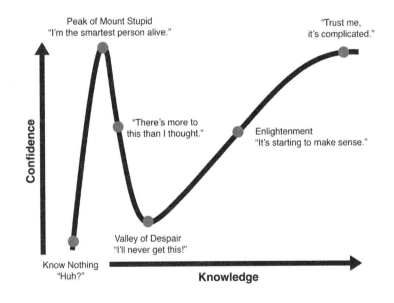

The Dunning-Kruger Effect Curve

At the bottom-left edge of the Dunning-Kruger curve is someone who knows nothing about the subject but has the self-awareness to know they know nothing. Many first-time leaders start here. But as someone begins to learn more about a difficult subject (such as leadership), a real problem occurs. They believe they know much more than they do. This is the second point on the chart: the peak of Mount Stupid.

People at the peak of Mount Stupid make terrible decisions and give bad advice. The investigation into the Space Shuttle Challenger disaster found that this cognitive bias explained how incompetent managers ignored the advice of their engineers, approving the use of the O-rings that ultimately failed, causing the explosion that destroyed the Shuttle and killed its seven crew members.

Are you guilty of the Dunning-Kruger effect in your own leadership? I sure was, sitting right up there on the top of Mount Stupid. Leadership is extremely hard to get right. If you aren't constantly learning and growing as a leader, and if you think you've "made it," there's a good chance you're overestimating your abilities.

But many frontline leaders have the opposite problem. After some initial excitement when they first step into their leadership role, they get stuck. They lack confidence in their power or ability to make change and effectively lead their teams. These leaders feel overwhelmed and at the mercy of the "chain of command," operational constraints, and unreasonable customer demands, which cause them to throw up their hands and say, "Nothing I do makes a difference anyway." These leaders are in the Valley of Despair on the Dunning-Kruger curve.

That's where I was after those initial talks with my friend Nate—I quickly toppled from the peak of Mount Stupid to the Valley of Despair. Many of the frontline leaders we've supported over the years are in the same dark spot. They feel lonely and helpless. They lose hope and don't think anything they can do will really make a difference.

Wherever you find yourself on the Dunning-Kruger curve and no matter your particular leadership situation, I want you to know that you *can* make a difference. I've seen it happen countless times over the years, and more recently, I've seen it in myself. I don't claim to have "solved" leadership, and I don't think of myself as an "expert" like I did before 2019. But I do think of myself as a guide. I have traveled the path I'm about to reveal to you. I know that if you make these mindset shifts, it will transform your relationships, your connections, and your impact.

FOUR MINDSET CHANGES TO MAKING THE LEADER-SHIFT

I love to hike. Being out in nature, on a trail, clears my head and gives me space to connect some dots. The thing I enjoy most about hiking is that every hike is different. Even if you are hiking a trail you've hiked before, something about the experience will be different. It might be the weather. You might have to detour because of a fallen tree or water running across a normally dry path. Depending on the time of year (or even the time of day), parts of the trail might be obscured.

Some days a hike is a pleasant walk in the woods. Other days, it's miserable. This happens regardless of how well you dress, pack, or prepare for circumstances on the trail. Even the most equipped hiker has to improvise sometimes. This is how I think about leadership.

Leadership is profoundly complicated. There are as many prescriptions for how to do it as there are people who write and talk about it. Like preparing for a hike, you can map out a strategy and pack some tools to take along the way. The practical tools I've found useful to me and to leaders we've helped over the years are what you'll see throughout this book.

But just like on a hike, conditions can change rapidly, and even the best-laid plans can go awry. The leadership tools and practices that worked for me or worked for others may not work for you in your specific situation or with your specific team. Your exact journey is not going to be the same as mine. It won't be the same as the one taken by your peer leaders, and it won't be the same as your mentors'. Each journey is cocreated by the unique circumstances of your business, your team, and your situation.

Even though the day-to-day conditions and teammates might change, there are some fundamental guideposts that apply to every journey. Most hiking trails have markings called "blazes" (as in "to blaze a trail"), which are periodic markers to tell you you're on the right path. If you look up and see a blaze, you know you're heading in the right direction. If you haven't seen a blaze in a while, it's time to stop and make sure you're still on the right track.

This book is about four critical mindset shifts that are the key "blazes" every leader needs to look for on their leadership journey. Those shifts are:

The 1st Shift: Believe in Your Impact
You Are Making a Difference (But What Kind?)
The 2nd Shift: Believe in Yourself
Tap into Your True Potential (and Your Biases)
The 3rd Shift: Believe in Others
Everyone Wants to Be Great (They Just Need to Believe)
The 4th Shift: Believe in Your Relationships
Moving Past the Phoniness (and Really Connecting)

I devote one chapter to each shift. In these chapters I explain how I experienced the four shifts in my own leadership and team, and I talk about the difference they've made for other successful leaders we've trained. I offer specific tools and practices to get you started, with the intention that you'll focus on these four "blazes" as you make your way along the path.

In addition to the Dunning-Kruger effect (now an inside joke anytime someone on our team wants to bring a colleague back down to earth), you'll learn:

- What the placebo effect and its lesser-known evil twin, the nocebo effect, teach leaders about the power of our assumptions

- How to "check yourself" and interrupt subconscious assumptions and beliefs you have about those you lead

- Simple ways to establish psychological safety and create real connection using the three questions of Approachable Leaders

- A leadership "judo move" that helps repair a strained relationship and build connection with your team

- Real-life work benefits like lower turnover, reduced stress, and improved performance, plus benefits at home like making more money, living longer and happier, and even an improved love life (it's true!)

- How to keep going when you're not sure it's working using tools like "anticipated acceptance" (kind of a "fake it till you make it" for leadership) to improve your life

A final chapter, "Make It Happen: Settling In, Dealing with Setbacks, and Bringing Others Along," is dedicated to ways to stay on the path, including how to overcome common obstacles and how to stay motivated when the trail gets rough.

WHY NOW? AND WHY YOU? A CRITICAL BEHAVIOR FOR TODAY'S LEADERS

The message about these four leadership shifts—and the need for them—couldn't be more relevant than it is today. We're in a period of leadership transition that we haven't seen since the post–World War II economic boom. We are just emerging from a pandemic that massively altered the labor market. The surge in senior leaders and staff leaving the workplace is unprecedented.

Millions of baby boomer and early Gen X leaders who were expected to work another decade or more are gone and are not coming back, at least not to the leadership roles they left behind. Much of the research we're seeing shows that older workers are leaning heavily into the gig economy, with the Pew Research Center estimating that 20 percent of gig workers in the United States are "over the age of fifty, and nearly a third of those are over the age of sixty-five."[3]

This leaves companies with a giant vacuum of experience needed for leadership development and a massive need for new people to fill the void. Most of those boomers and Gen Xers who left the market would have acted as mentors to younger leaders. Not anymore.

Compounding this is another thing that got revolutionized by the pandemic—the way we communicate. Tons of work is done remotely on Zoom and Teams. On the plus side, this creates flexibility and work-life opportunities never before possible. But it also generates a huge set of challenges for leaders, especially new or struggling ones. A lot of the nuances of body language and expressions are lost on Zoom, and lost with them are opportunities to create connection and psychological safety. If you are around somebody face-to-face every day, it's easier to build a relationship and fix occasional mistakes. These factors increase pressure on young leaders even more.

Younger people also expect much more from their workplace. And because they are in such high demand, they often get what they ask for. This includes things like a healthy work-life balance, an environment where they can show up as their full selves, and quick (if not immediate) growth opportunities. It's not that companies don't want to provide these things, but the reality often can be far from the expectation, and there is little patience for anything that doesn't immediately gratify these expectations.

This creates an almost impossible pressure-cooker environment for leaders. As companies struggle to fill roles, leaders are expected to manage larger teams (often including remote workers) with little or no support. It's a volatile environment where new and inexperienced leaders are forced to figure it out on their own—and in a hurry.

I've been focusing on younger leaders, but this exact same challenge impacts experienced leaders who grew their skill set in a very different environment. What may have worked in the past with a previous workforce doesn't work today. Those leaders undergo a separate kind of frustration. They'll remember their previous success and blame younger workers for their lack of experience.

"These kids just don't understand how the world works," the seasoned leaders say. "They expect too much, and there's no way to please them." This quickly turns this older generation—my generation—against younger workers. We throw up our hands in frustration, and in doing so, we create a stressful and problematic work environment.

This massively changed labor market creates challenges wherever you are on the leadership spectrum. What used to work doesn't anymore. And today you don't really have the luxury of time to build up a lot of experience.

Leaders today don't get a chance to learn what works and what doesn't. They just get punished when they screw up. Often mistakes get compounded by the added stress of stepping in to do the work of a person who just left. It creates an extremely stressful, high-consequence environment for younger leaders. It's unfair. And it raises the stakes on rapidly developing the basics of leadership.

WHY *THIS* BOOK?

You can see that I'm passionate about the four leadership shifts, but I know you might still be skeptical and wonder why you should be excited about this journey. With all the leadership books written each year, why read this one?

There are as many leadership theories as there are leadership consultants. Our clients don't hire us for what works in theory. They hire us to see actual improvements in their cultures and results. While we've done the research (especially research on how our own training impacts results on the ground with our clients), my number one goal anytime I talk to a leader is the *practical takeaway*. What will you do differently when you walk out of our training? What new actions will you be inspired to take when you put down this book?

In addition to what I've learned on my own leadership journey, this book crystallizes the in-depth research and learning we've distilled during our workshops and coaching that have transformed the work lives of tens of thousands of leaders. Over this time, I've learned that the most effective, positive, and sustainable leadership starts with a belief in your own potential as a leader and in the potential of everyone you lead.

Beliefs influence behavior, which directly impacts your culture and the growth and development (or not) of the people on your team. That's the bottom line of this book. I want to inspire you to shift your beliefs so you can be your best and reach your highest potential, and your teammates and organization can do the same.

My assumption about you is that you want to be a great leader— otherwise you wouldn't have picked up this book. My hope is that you will commit to not just reading the book but also to applying the practical tools in your work and personal life. Start with yourself. Embrace the four mindset shifts, and they will transform the way you lead yourself and the way you lead others.

Everyone dreams of being great. The part they need help with is believing they can be. I believe in you. I believe you are great, and I know you have all it takes to be an outstanding leader. This book will show you how.

YOUR TURN: WHO'S YOUR HERO LEADER? (YOUR FIRST ASSIGNMENT)

Before we go any further, I've got some news. You've got homework. You're not going to change your leadership just sitting there reading about it. So this book includes some assignments. (Don't worry—they're not TOO hard.)

This first assignment is one of my favorite exercises from our workshops. You'll read a story about it later, but I want you to try it now.

PART A

Step 1. Think about someone who was an important leader in your life. Who first comes to mind when you hear the words *great leader*? Ideally think of a work leader, but this could also be someone in your personal life (a pastor, coach, parent, or teacher).

Step 2. After you've thought about WHO your leader is, write their name below and then write WHY you chose this person.

Steps 3 and 4. Next, list TWO BEHAVIORS you admire about their leadership. Remember, a behavior is a *visible* way this person acted, something you can *observe*. You can't say, "They trusted me," or "They respected me." Those are your conclusions. Instead, describe what they actually did: "They let me do things my own way before jumping in," or "They always asked me for my opinion." What did they do well as a leader?

Once you've written down the four items below, continue to part B.

LEADER'S NAME	
WHY YOU PICKED THEM	
BEHAVIOR ONE	
BEHAVIOR TWO	

PART B

There are two things to think about and do with the leader you just picked.

Step 1. Consider the behaviors you just wrote down. Guess what? These leadership behaviors don't just describe the person you chose as your leader. They also describe yourself. We tend to project the behaviors we admire in ourselves onto others. The behaviors you admire in your leader are actually behaviors you admire in yourself.

Look at the two behaviors you listed. On your best leadership days, you probably demonstrate these behaviors. On your worst leadership days, you probably don't do these as well.

Step 2. Contact your leader today. (If the person you picked is no longer living, I want you to reach out to someone who knew them.) Tell the person you contact what your leader meant to you and why.

The leader you chose had a powerful influence on you, and you can have that same influence on the people you lead. Wouldn't it be great if we could give others experiences like that every day? How cool would it be if we could "bottle up" those moments and deliver them whenever we wanted?

Changing your leadership mindset using the four shifts will help you do just that.

YOU ARE MAKING A DIFFERENCE (BUT WHAT KIND?)

"We do not see things as they are, we see them as we are."
—Anais Nin

You know how they say even therapists need a therapist? I guess the same is true for leadership consultants.

While Nate rejected my offer to join our team as my chief of staff, he did agree to help us implement a new "operating system" for the firm.[1] He held our hands through the major work of transitioning the company from dysfunctional but surviving to healthy and thriving.

A key part of implementing the updated operating system was creating a new role called *integrator*, the person who would be my copilot in running the company. I considered who could handle the new responsibility and realized that Debbie, a member of our team for close to fifteen years, would be perfect for the role. I naively assumed that she'd be excited for the new leadership position and the chance to run the company with me. What an honor I was bestowing! But I was still on the top of Mount Stupid.

When I excitedly told Debbie about the opportunity, she looked back at me, a little uncomfortable. "I have to tell you something," she said, "and I don't think you're going to like it. . . . I told your dad that he couldn't retire until I was ready to retire, because I would *never* work for you."

Ouch. Not the answer I expected.

Debbie was reluctant to take on the role for all the same reasons our company was stuck in the first place. She thought this new system was just another shiny object I was chasing. She didn't think I really had faith in her or the rest of the team. She was concerned that everyone else would be skeptical of the process, given my behavior over the years. Oh, and I drove her crazy.

There were a lot of difficult conversations over the course of convincing Debbie to become our integrator, not the least of which was me proving to her that this wasn't a shiny object and I was serious. We talked a lot about the things I did that drove her and the rest of the team nuts and vice versa (hey, nobody's perfect . . . not even Debbie). In this new system, my role is called *visionary*, and I asked Debbie to read a book called *Rocket Fuel* that discusses how common it is for visionaries and integrators to make each other a little crazy. It described us both perfectly.

Debbie ultimately agreed to accept the role (thank goodness—

it's transformed our culture and our company). But I had to concede a number of things before she would trust me and believe I was truly committed. I even agreed that she could remove me from the leadership team if I wasn't following through on my commitments!

I had no clue about how my behavior as a leader was impacting my relationships with my team, our culture, and our results. Debbie's reaction helped me understand for the first time the impact I was having on those around me. It was a tough wake-up call.

I'd always seen myself as a good leader. I had led our company through some incredibly tough times, and on the backside of those problems, we'd set records for performance. Heck, I traveled the country teaching a leadership framework that I'd developed, and it was changing lives!

But here I was confronting the fact that not only was I *not* some superstar leader, I was causing our dysfunction. I felt like a fraud. This was the beginning of a number of tough and necessary conversations—first with the leadership team and then with the rest of the company. And our company and our culture have never been stronger in our more than forty-year history.

WHAT KIND OF AN IMPACT ARE YOU HAVING AS A LEADER? THE NOCEBO EFFECT

You're probably familiar with the placebo effect, a mind-body reaction where patients who believe they are receiving treatment for a symptom will experience relief, even when they aren't actually getting treatment. In medical trials, half of the patients get a sugar pill instead of the new drug. Many patients who receive the sugar pill report experiencing the same relief promised by the new medicine.

The placebo effect also shows up in sham surgeries. Patients who believe they received a surgical treatment (but didn't) also see their symptoms improve. The study that blows my mind is one where half the patients received a sham knee surgery (just an incision and stitches but no other treatment) and recovered just as well as the patients who underwent the full orthopedic operation![2] In many cases, the sugar pills or sham surgeries actually *outperform* the treatment being tested. (Those treatments don't get approved.)

The nocebo effect is the placebo effect's evil twin. In this case, if you give someone a sugar pill and tell them it's a drug with certain side effects, a significant number of patients will experience those side effects. The nocebo effect is a serious medical problem.

One study found that women who believed they were at risk of heart disease were four times more likely to die than similarly situated women who didn't think they were at risk.[3] In another, patients who learned about the muscle pain side effects of taking statins began reporting muscle pain at a much higher rate than normal (muscle pain does happen but is extremely rare). These patients then stopped taking their cholesterol medicine. Thousands of people die every year from heart attacks they would have avoided if they had just continued to take their statins.[4]

The most extreme version of the nocebo effect is voodoo death.[5] First coined by Walter Cannon in 1942, voodoo death is a sudden physical decline that occurs after a subject strongly believes that they have been cursed (often by a "witch doctor"). Under the right set of circumstances, an otherwise normal and healthy person can convince their body to experience a rapid decline and, in some cases, even die. It is literally a death caused by the nocebo effect. These deaths have been reported by anthropologists for years and are especially prevalent in cultures that believe strongly in the supernatural.

The nocebo effect creates an ethical dilemma for doctors. A doctor is ethically required to tell patients about the potential negative side effects of a treatment. But, because of the nocebo effect, mentioning the side effects could cause the patient to experience them when they otherwise wouldn't. And, as in the case of the statins, it may even discourage them from receiving life-saving treatment.

One way doctors are working around this problem is to ask patients up front for permission to only mention side effects if or when specifically asked. The doctor and patient stay in close contact as the treatment begins so the doctor can monitor for the side effects without necessarily disclosing them.

LEADERS AND THE NOCEBO EFFECT

Wondering what the nocebo effect and voodoo death have to do with your leadership? A lot.

I spent years as a nocebo effect leader with my own team. I would hold meetings with the team about some new idea, and everyone would leave excited about the project. Then I would do it myself or decide it wasn't a priority and let it die on the vine. I was like a doctor telling my team there would be a lot of negative side effects if I relied on them. And that's exactly the culture I was creating.

Now I try hard to be a placebo effect leader. I encourage the team, and we spend a lot of time celebrating wins. When things don't go as expected, we don't dwell on the failure. Instead, we look ahead to what we can learn to do better in the future. Over the last four years, we have moved people around and asked them to take on new roles and responsibilities. We've asked them to stretch, learn, and grow.

What kind of leader are you? Do you focus on the problems or look for solutions? If someone stumbles, do you concentrate on how they failed or how this can be a learning opportunity? Do you encourage your team to try new things or discourage them from getting too far out of their box?

As a leader, you are like that doctor advising the patient. The things you say or the way you behave (based on your assumptions) will affect how your people respond. When you believe in your team and encourage them, you create the placebo effect. When you don't trust your team and deter them from a sense of ownership, you create the nocebo effect. You can very literally "voodoo curse" your teammates to failure.

The tools and practices in this book are not just about leadership at work. You can trigger the nocebo effect with your spouse, your family, and in the case of voodoo curses, even your own body. You really can't afford to be a nocebo effect leader.

IS YOUR GLASS HALF-EMPTY?

"There are only two mantras, yum and yuck. Mine is yum."
—TOM ROBBINS

Some people think the lemonade glass is always half-full. Others see the glass as half-empty. Then there was my father-in-law, may he rest in peace. He was more of an "Is that lemonade or a urine sample?" kind of guy.

When my wife and I found out we were pregnant with our daughter, we were excited to tell her mom and dad. They lived in Florida, so we had to deliver the news by phone. We figured Janet should be the one to tell them. That was our first mistake—she was nervous, and her parents weren't always the easiest to talk with. Her dad answered the phone. Starting with him was our second mistake. He was an engineer and really smart but sometimes a little slow on the uptake when it came to people stuff.

Janet jumped right in. She made sure her mom was in earshot so they could both hear at the same time, which made things a little awkward from the start. Then she got right to it—sort of. "Well, Phil and I wanted to let you know that I took a pregnancy test. And it came back . . ." Insert awkward silence.

I've only had one chance to do a pregnancy reveal, but if I had to do it over again, I wouldn't bury the lead by talking about the pregnancy test, because at the end of the awkward silence, Janet just blurted out, "POSITIVE!" Her mom, who was listening in the background, immediately figured out what was happening and started screaming. Her dad confusedly asked, "Positive for *what?*"

I'm not sure what other conditions her dad thought pregnancy tests identified, but he was definitely thinking more about the urine sample than the full glass!

Nocebo effect leaders are a lot like my father-in-law, always looking at the glass half-empty (or worse). It's easy to do. Leaders today—especially frontline leaders—often feel powerless. Squeezed between demands from above and below, they don't believe they can make a real difference in the lives of those they lead.

Frustrated, stretched thin, and often burned out, they assume the worst about their teammates. They watch their team like a hawk, waiting for a screwup they know is bound to happen. They habitually look at the glass half-empty. Some days it's lemonade and other days . . . well, you get the picture.

Most leaders don't want to be glass half-empty types, whose approach reinforces a terrible "race to the bottom" culture. They want something more. They want to reap the benefits of their hard work and see their teammates thrive. They want to feel like they matter, and they do.

Before I started writing my last book, I spent a couple of years asking anyone who would listen to me this question: "What do you think is the most important difference between a good leader and a bad one?" I called this the search for the "one leadership ring to rule them all" (yeah, I'm a nerd).

One day a friend of mine replied, "You know, I'm not sure this is the one ring, but a mentor of mine taught me this test that would immediately tell him whether someone had what it takes to be a good manager." I was all ears.

"He would have the potential manager imagine that a coworker comes up and makes a factual statement they know is flat-out wrong," she explained, "something every employee should know. And then he'd ask them, 'What's the first thing that comes into your head?'"

Take a second and imagine this yourself.

What comes up? Is your first instinct to correct their mistake?

To tell them what they got wrong? Did you wonder how they could be so off base? Deep down, did you think they might not be that bright? That's the mantra of yuck. That's the nocebo effect leader (or as we'll learn about in the next chapter, a leader making the "villain assumption").

Placebo effect leaders see the glass half-full and choose the mantra of yum. That's what my friend's mentor was looking for in good managers. They handle situations like these with curiosity. They wonder, "What are they seeing that I'm not seeing?" They ask questions. "Does this person have the facts right?" A yum leader is open to the idea that maybe they're the one who needs to adjust something. They try to learn.

Yum leaders see a world of possibility and abundance, not a zero-sum world of limitation and scarcity. Their assumption is *always* that their teammates are smart, capable, and on top of things. When they look at their teammates, they think *yum* not *yuck*.

When a yum leader sees a teammate struggling, they see it as a chance to remind them of their talent and how they've overcome obstacles in the past. It's a time to remind them that you believe in them, and then pitch in to help in any way you can. Leaders who think *yuck* see this as the failure of someone who just doesn't "get it."

A nocebo effect boss sees someone going above and beyond and thinks, *Yuck, this go-getter is going to show me up or expect some favor in return.* A placebo effect leader thinks, *Yum,* and makes sure this contribution is noticed, celebrated, and appreciated. They make a mental note to remind their teammate of this success in the future when an obstacle gets in their way.

THEORY X AND THEORY Y

A fancier way to think about the glass half-empty versus half-full leader is Theory X and Theory Y, two contrasting approaches to leadership first proposed by the legendary organizational development professor Douglas McGregor in the 1960s.[6]

Theory X leaders think people are inherently lazy and don't like to work (they think yuck or glass half-empty). They think employees generally lack ambition and resist change. Because of this, they need a lot of controls in place to make sure they perform their role, and they must be watched closely. Theory X managers, therefore, rely on rules, punishment, and a top-down approach to management.

The other view—Theory Y—assumes that employees are self-motivated to do a good job and try their best (they think yum or glass half-full). They believe employees want to learn and grow and will take responsibility and work hard with their teammates to accomplish big goals. When employees struggle, a Theory Y manager doesn't blame the worker or micromanage. Instead, she looks for the obstacles getting in the way.

Like yum and yuck, Theory X and Y represent two different mindsets leaders have about team members. Your mindset will determine how you approach motivation, delegation, communication, and performance management. Theory Y managers are much more likely to deal with problems by collaborating with the team, asking for suggestions, and helping teammates grow and develop. I'm obviously a big fan of Theory Y.

YOUR TURN: VOTE FOR Y

Most leaders aren't always a yum or always a yuck. Or they might be a yum toward some teammates and a yuck toward others. If you want to be more of a Theory Y leader, a good place to start is to begin paying attention to how often you are a yum and how often you are a yuck during your day.

A good way to think about this is casting votes. Each time you treat a teammate as a yum, that's a vote for Y. If you treat an employee as a yuck, you've cast a vote for X. How many votes can you cast for Theory Y during your workday?

Over the next week or so, complete a daily vote tally for your leadership interactions. Write down each interaction you had with your team and then honestly reflect on whether that interaction was a vote for Theory X or a vote for Theory Y.

Theory Y Votes Who? Context?	Theory X Votes Who? Context?

Some things to look out for here include:

- How many overall votes do you have each day? If you have a hard time listing items, this could be a sign that you aren't very available to your team.

- Are your votes almost all for Theory Y? You might be a total Theory Y leader, in which case I applaud you. But it's safe to say that most leaders (even, for example, the one writing this book) can easily slip into Theory X from time to time. If you don't have any votes for Theory X during the day, reflect on whether you are being fully self-aware. Are you at the top of Mount Stupid?

- Consider going over your vote tally with a trusted peer, especially if they happened to have witnessed some of the interactions you listed for that day. See if they agree with your tally or your assessment.

Challenge yourself to cast those votes and reflect each day on how many examples of Theory Y votes you can recall.

YOUR TURN: WWYD?

Being a glass half-empty leader is just a habit of thinking, and habits can change. James Clear, in his terrific book *Atomic Habits*, argues that our habits reflect our current identity. Therefore, to make a habit stick, you also must make sure your identity is consistent with the habit you want to create. For example, he suggests that people who've identified as an unhealthy or overweight person their whole life have to work hard to shift to a healthy identity.[7]

Clear suggests going throughout your day asking the question, "What would a healthy person do?" That helps you quickly filter each decision through a healthy identity. You won't have to ask for long, because soon you will adopt the identity of a healthy person.

You can do the same thing in your day-to-day leadership. As you go through your day, ask yourself, "What would a Theory

Y leader do?" (or "What would Y do?" for short). That way, you can filter decisions through the Theory Y identity as you move through your day.

One practice I use to help cement this habit is called the "Three Happys" in my daily journal. Most mornings I jot down three things from the day before that made me happy. I regularly include at least one conversation or interaction with someone on my team. This practice does two things. First, it's an easy way to capture some of my "votes for Y" that happened the day before. Second, and even more important, it gets my brain in the habit of looking for "votes for Y" during my day.

Try to review your own daily interactions this way. Pretty soon you'll be casting a lot of votes for Theory Y, and your team will notice.

TAP INTO YOUR TRUE POTENTIAL (AND YOUR BIASES)

*"At the moment of commitment the entire
universe conspires to ensure your success."*
—**Johann Wolfgang von Goethe**

WHAT'S YOUR STORY (ABOUT YOUR OWN POTENTIAL)?

How do you see yourself as a leader? You may be like I was and think you're doing a good job. Or you may feel like you have leadership potential but need some more work. Maybe you're not sure you have what it takes to be a leader in the first place. What's your personal leadership story?

Since you're reading a book on leadership, I assume you believe you have *some* potential as a leader. If you believe that, I have great news: that belief in your potential is the foundation of a strong leader.

What if you aren't sure about your leadership potential? Congratulations! I have more great news: your uncertainty also says a lot about your leadership potential. Remember the Dunning-Kruger effect and how I thought I was a great leader? It was only after I recognized the damage I was causing that I was able to make the shifts I needed to transform the culture of my own team.

YOUR LEADERSHIP IDENTITY

Your leadership at its most basic is simply how you behave toward your team each day. Those day-to-day actions are based on your beliefs about yourself and your team. Thinking this way, leadership is really just a habit of thinking. If you want to change or improve your leadership, then your habits must change. Habits are basically subroutines that run automatically throughout our lives and follow a certain pattern.

James Clear argues that our habits reflect our current identity. Therefore, to make a new habit stick, you must make sure your identity is consistent with the habit you want to create.

My own leadership transformation started after I was confronted with examples of how my behavior was damaging my team and my company. Before then, I saw myself as a take-charge type of leader who, when confronted by a challenge, would roll up my sleeves and just handle it myself. I didn't trust my team to do things the way I wanted or as fast as I wanted, so I didn't delegate much, and even when I did, I would often do my own version of the work. I took pride in all the plates I could keep spinning.

Over time, my leadership identity has changed. Now I take pride in seeing my team learn and grow. I delegate much more, and I trust my team to hold themselves and one another accountable. I regularly seek feedback about what I can do to improve as a leader. My identity changed from a Theory X place of superiority to a Theory Y place of humility. That change in identity led to big differences in my day-to-day behavior, which in turn changed how the whole team behaved toward me and toward one another.

What kind of identity do you have as a leader?

FINDING A DIFFERENT MANTRA: THE PATTERN INTERRUPT

A mantra often refers to a repeated sound used during meditation to aid in concentration. But a mantra is anything you repeat to yourself, either consciously or subconsciously. That's why a yum or yuck mindset can be thought of as a mantra.

If you find yourself in a yuck or glass half-empty frame of mind more often than you'd like, you need a different mantra. Since you're probably not planning on a meditation retreat in the mountains anytime soon, here is a different strategy: the pattern interrupt.

Do you remember where you were on September 11, 2001?

I happened to be with my wife, Janet, at a Tony Robbins conference in Hawaii on September 11. That may sound like a good place to be stranded for a week, but it was scary. Yeah, we were in paradise. But like the rest of the world, we had no idea exactly what was going on, and we also had no idea of when we were ever going to make it back home.

Here's a couple of pictures of me from that day:

There were a lot of unforgettable things about that week. Those pictures above are from when I climbed to the top of a telephone pole and took a selfie (using an actual camera with film—this was nearly twenty years before your phone took pictures). I walked on hot coals and lived to tell the tale. But the thing I remember most from that week was the "pattern interrupt."

A pattern interrupt short-circuits a routine and triggers your brain to step out of a predetermined habit loop. For example, during the event, if someone said, "I don't understand," Robbins would literally get the entire room to cheer. Why? Most people are afraid to ask questions in a ballroom full of people. Robbins wanted the crowd to contribute and volunteer questions. His pattern interrupt reversed the normal habit and led people to do exactly the opposite.

How can you put the pattern interrupt to work for you? Let's say you're like me and occasionally find yourself slipping back into Theory X (old habits die hard!). Maybe you have a teammate who makes mistakes when they get busy and today you notice another one.

You catch yourself thinking, *There they go again—they really need to pay closer attention!* You realize that your first reaction is that they messed up because they are the type of person who doesn't pay attention to details. You cast a vote for Theory X.

What if you wanted to take your vote back? You can use a pattern interrupt similar to the one Tony Robbins used. When you witness an employee making a mistake, you could interrupt the pattern. "This is awesome! What a great learning opportunity!" This may sound a little contrived, but trust me, it works.

One habit we've had as an organization is me chasing shiny objects (I tell a recent story about this in "The 4th Shift"). I really try to not send people down these rabbit trails, but I still slip up from time to time. That's why we've asked the team to tell me to "get back in my box" when I ask them to divert from something they're working on to chase whatever has caught my attention.

Whenever someone tells me to get back in my box, I make a *huge* deal about it. People don't normally expect a celebration for telling their boss no. But we want to reinforce this behavior, and by interrupting the normal pattern, I am reinforcing how important I take this commitment. It's always done in a fun way, but it makes the point that we are committed to changing this habit. The whole point is to make sure your brain is now looking for opportunities to run the Theory Y pattern versus the Theory X pattern.

ARE YOU BIASED? DON'T SAY NO UNTIL YOU IMAGINE THIS

One common reason leaders can default to yuck or Theory X is because of bias. I'm not talking about discrimination. But we all make subconscious assumptions about others around us, and those beliefs impact the way we act toward others. We're biased. Don't think you're biased? Imagine this scenario:

You're driving to work. Sipping your coffee. Listening to your favorite podcast. At the most traffic-jammed intersection of your drive, someone squeezes in between you and the car just ahead. How do you feel? Right. What a jerk!

Now imagine you stop for gas. You try pulling out of the convenience store into the same intersection. And what happens? Nobody will let you merge. After fuming for three minutes, you jam your way in, causing someone to hit their brakes (and salute you). Now how do you feel? Right again. What a bunch of jerks!

You see yourself as the hero of both driving stories, overcoming all those villains on the roadways. But are you always an angel in the car? Yeah, me neither.[1]

People tend to view their own behavior in the best light possible. When we react to something (like traffic), we explain our behavior based on the situation. But the behavior of others? That's a different story. We explain other people's behavior based on traits. This is called actor-observer bias (or fundamental attribution error, if you want to get real fancy-schmancy). And it is just one cognitive bias that impacts your leadership.[2]

HOW WE *REALLY* MAKE DECISIONS

One of the best books I've read in the last decade is *Thinking, Fast and Slow* by Daniel Kahneman,[3] the only social psychologist to win the Nobel Prize in economics. It summarizes the groundbreaking research that Kahneman did with his close friend Amos Tversky, who would have shared the prize except they don't award them posthumously. Their research shattered the foundational assumption that humans make economically rational decisions. Instead, Kahneman and Tversky prove in study after study that humans make decisions using two different systems of thinking: System 1 and System 2.

System 1 is fast, automatic, and unconscious. We use System 1 for most of our daily decisions. It works well for making quick judgments based on limited information. Without System 1, functioning well in our lives would be impossible. However, System 1 often acts on emotion and regularly makes irrational decisions to avoid perceived potential pain or loss.

System 2 is deliberative and takes more time and mental effort. We use System 2 for complex, out-of-the-ordinary tasks (like math, analyzing, and making complicated decisions). System 2 is valuable for these tasks but makes mistakes, especially if we are tired or overworked. System 2 is more likely to behave like a rational economic actor.

Kahneman and Tversky argue that we are biased to use System 1, even when we should use System 2, and this often leads to poor decisions. System 1 leads to actor-observer bias, where people attribute their own bad behavior to external circumstances and other people's bad behavior to internal beliefs or motivation.

A COMMON LEADERSHIP BLIND SPOT

Bias is a leadership "blind spot" lurking in the background. It's rarely overt or even conscious. It's implicit and hidden from plain sight. A great book on implicit bias is *Blindspot: Hidden Biases of Good People* by Mahzarin R. Banaji and Anthony G. Greenwald. Their main message is that we all experience bias:

> A quarter century ago, most psychologists believed that human behavior was primarily guided by conscious thoughts and feelings. Nowadays the majority will readily agree that *much of human judgment and behavior is produced with little conscious thought* (emphasis added).[4]

Just like professors Khaneman and Tversky found, although we like to think we act based on logic, we rarely do. We tend to automatically prefer people who look like us or share similar backgrounds. In the case of actor-observer bias, we take it one step further. We prefer people who *are* us. And since we don't think we're biased, we never turn on System 2 and question our decision-making.

Banaji and Greenwald find we often react to things without even thinking about them. It's automatic. They continue:

> Eric Kandel, a neuroscientist at Columbia University who received a Nobel Prize for his work on memory, was once pressed to say how much of the mind works unconsciously; he gave an estimate of 80 to 90 percent. John Bargh, a psychologist at Yale University, isn't bashful about putting the number at Ivory soap's 99 and 44/100 percent.[5]

Every day we unconsciously react to people and situations based on biases we don't realize we have. Or worse, biases we tell ourselves we don't have.

THREE WAYS TO OVERCOME YOUR OWN BIAS AS A LEADER

We rarely think about our biases because we don't want to think about them. It's hard. Many of us believe we aren't biased, despite our actions telling a different story. The Russian novelist Fyodor Dostoevsky calls these "colorless lies" because they are lies we don't even reveal to ourselves.

The fact is that our biases run the show more often than we realize. And that's a problem. Because if we operate on autopilot, our behavior won't change. But once you shine a light on bias, you give yourself an opportunity to begin questioning your assumptions and interrupt negative patterns. Here are three research-backed ways you can manage your bias:

I. CHECK YOURSELF (BEFORE YOU WRECK YOURSELF)

Step one is to switch off the autopilot occasionally. Professor Banaji and another colleague created numerous tests that reveal implicit bias. If you feel like doing some self-awareness work, I encourage you to check out the Implicit Association Tests.[6] They were very eye-opening for me—and my family.

The Implicit Association Tests focus mainly on traits like race, culture, age, and gender. Knowing your implicit bias in these areas is obviously very important. But one version of the test looks at bias between flowers and insects. While it is good to understand specific biases, the bigger point is just to understand that we are all biased. It gives you a road map for situations when you should engage your System 2 thinking and question implicit assumptions about others.

You also need to check for cognitive bias like the actor-observer bias and confirmation bias, another bug in your cognitive operating system.[7] You are hardwired to ignore information that disagrees with your beliefs, and you'll pay closer attention to and overweigh evidence in favor of your beliefs. This means the System 1 operating system is wired to judge others more harshly (actor-observer bias) and to look for evidence that agrees with our harsh conclusions about them (confirmation bias). We will also ignore evidence that might make us question our harsh judgment.

We all have biases, and we rarely question whether those are impacting our decisions or behavior (spoiler alert: they are). Once you understand your potential bias, you're more likely to trigger System 2 and interrupt a potentially negative pattern. To do that, you move to step two.

2. TEACH YOURSELF TO TURN OFF (AND SOMETIMES TURN ON) YOUR AUTOPILOT

Our implicit or cognitive bias doesn't happen in a vacuum. It's situational. It occurs when we make a decision or respond to an event. These are "triggers," and each one is an opportunity to question (or act based on) bias. For example, consider these situations:

- Someone with an accent applies for a customer service job. You don't think they'll be a good fit. Why? You don't think your customers will accept talking to someone with an accent.

- A small person asks to be a helper in your fabrication shop. You immediately push them to the "no" pile. Why? There's a lot of heavy lifting involved that this person probably can't handle.

- One of your teammates seems to spend a lot of time on TikTok. They come to you with an idea to reduce the amount of time it takes to do their operation. You internally roll your eyes, figuring they are just trying to get out of more work.

Each one of these might seem like a reasonable reaction. Sometimes language and weight restrictions rise to the level of actual job requirements. But we often don't question the assumptions behind these reactions. Any of them could be due to implicit or cognitive bias.

Maybe your customers will enjoy someone with an unusual accent. Or this could be an opportunity to reduce or eliminate heavy lifting in fabrication—not to mention, these days you never know who's lifting giant tires after work at the cross-fit gym! And the "lazy" employee might have just given you a huge money-saving idea. (Walter Chrysler is often credited with saying, "Whenever there is a hard job to be done I assign it to a lazy man; he is sure to find an easy way of doing it.") Some economists even argue that time on social media may mask huge productivity gains at work.[8]

HOW TO TURN OFF YOUR AUTOPILOT

In situations like these, use the trigger as a chance to question your assumptions. Your goal is to create cognitive dissonance[9] and get your System 2 (analytical) brain working. Our Leader-Shift Toolkit includes a Trigger Tool. It encourages leaders to reflect on these triggers. But here are three questions to get you started:

- What is our proof for the assumption? Is there any evidence that the opposite is true?

- Are there any resources or alternatives that could overcome the potential obstacle? Have we ever overcome a situation like this before?

- Is this an opportunity to rethink the way "we've always done" things? What new strategies could we create from this circumstance?

These questions will help get your brain off autopilot and nudge you to face any implicit or cognitive bias in an honest and productive way. This turns on System 2.

3. RESET YOUR AUTOPILOT

It's easy to get discouraged when you start thinking about implicit and cognitive bias. Leaders get the chance to act on bias dozens of times a day. And be honest: How often do you look at your employees like those drivers on the road I mentioned earlier? How often do you see them as a yuck?

Late for a meeting? Probably wasting time on social media. Quality issue? They must not care as much about the work as you do. Worse yet, you may be making these negative assumptions about yourself. Do you ever wonder whether you have what it takes to be a great leader? Are you organized enough? Driven enough?

The stereotypes and implicit assumptions we make negatively affect the way we act and behave toward ourselves and even harm our health.[10] One study Banaji and Greenwald cite shows that elderly people who have negative implicit assumptions about age are more likely to suffer from heart disease when they're older.

Being a Theory Y leader isn't just about being nice to yourself or the people on your team. It is a key difference maker in how everyone performs. As we'll see in the next chapter, your assumptions about your team influence their expectations and performance—for better or worse.

That's why step three is to work hard to make Theory Y your "default" position. Anytime you experience a trigger, look for how the glass is half-full. Assume positive intent. When your coworker reacts, think of them like the actor instead of the observer (the same way you would for yourself).

Each of us faces a complicated set of implicit and cognitive biases. We almost never think about them (after all, they're implicit). Even worse, they are very hard to overcome. At the same time, the actions we take on these assumptions have a powerful impact on ourselves and everyone around us. This means we must always look out for them and be ready to manage them when they pop up. You can do that by:

- Checking yourself (working on self-awareness and always being on the lookout for implicit and cognitive bias)

- Checking your autopilot (looking for triggering situations and creating alarms to make sure you consider bias; looking for situations where you can set your autopilot to overcome potential bias)

- Making Theory Y your "default" setting (setting you and your team up for success by assuming the best and not the worst)

I know you can do it. After all, I believe in you!

THE TAKEAWAY: YOUR POTENTIAL

Leadership is hard, and it can be lonely—especially for frontline leaders, who I think have the hardest job in any company. There is a lot of pressure from above ("Get the production out the door!"). There is a lot of pressure from below ("Do those guys upstairs have any idea how impossible this is?"). It's easy to tell yourself the story that you really don't have that much influence on things at work. Nothing could be further from the truth.

Frontline leaders have a massive influence on the day-to-day experience of their team, which translates to their performance. Many say, "Culture eats strategy for breakfast," and I agree. You are the builder of that culture. Culture isn't some poster on a wall or some statement in an employee handbook. Culture is literally the sum of daily experiences your team has with you and with one another. You define the culture. You are the actor, not the observer.

Your belief in your own potential impacts your assumptions about your team. Your assumptions about your team directly impact their behavior (for better or worse). Even though I'm cheering for you, this isn't a bunch of leadership rah-rah. The research conclusively shows that frontline leaders, far from being powerless, are powerful beyond imagination. In the next chapter, you'll learn why you don't have the luxury to believe anything else.

EVERYONE WANTS TO BE GREAT (THEY JUST NEED TO BELIEVE)

"If I accept you as you are, I make you worse;
however, if I treat you as though you are what you
are capable of becoming I help you become that."
—**Johann Wolfgang von Goethe**

"**N**o offense, but maybe I should talk to Laura," Debbie suggested. She was obviously nervous about how this conversation might go. "I think she'll take it better from me than you." And, of course, Debbie was right again (which was getting annoying).

Implementing a new operating system required a lot of changes. It started with looking hard at how to best organize the team to accomplish our goals. We had the right people, but we didn't have everyone in the right seat.

Laura had been with us for thirteen years in the same data entry position. Over the years her skills developed and she added responsibilities, but she was doing the same basic role that whole time. She did a great job, but she was firmly stuck in her "data entry box" on our accountability chart.

As Debbie's role grew, it became clear that we needed to move some things off her plate. Bookkeeping and accounts payable took up a lot of her time, and it made sense to delegate that to someone. Nobody on the team had that background, and we didn't really want to hire someone new.

After thinking about it, Debbie asked, "What about Laura?"

I wasn't sure. For me, Laura was still in the same data entry box she'd been in for more than a decade, but the longer I sat on it, the more I realized that Laura had started tiptoeing out of her box. In recent years, she'd volunteered to lead a company health initiative, along with participating in many of the community volunteer activities we did. She'd started leading our weekly all-hands meeting. But still, this seemed a little different. This was asking her to *really* step out of her box.

"I trust her to do it, and I think she's got everything she needs to handle the role," I responded, "but that's a pretty big change." Debbie and I both knew that Laura wasn't big on change. "I'm not sure how she'd handle something so new."

We agreed that Debbie would talk to her first, and she confirmed that our hunch was correct: Laura was nervous about the change. She wasn't sure she could do the role, and she was uncomfortable with having that much responsibility. Debbie told her we both believed in her and wanted her to try it.

I talked to Laura later. She shared that she was worried about losing her job if she moved out of her old role and then wasn't able to perform to our standards. I reassured her that was not going to happen. I asked her to look at it like an experiment. Debbie and I were confident she'd do great, but if not, she could go back to the data entry role.

It wasn't an easy transition. Data entry in accounting is a lot different from what Laura was doing in our databases. She had to learn new software. She needed to pick up a lot of new accounting knowledge. And she remained nervous about the job. One day I came into her office to hand her a bonus check. After I handed her the envelope, she looked up at me.

"What is it?" she asked.

"A bonus check—we had a great quarter," I replied.

"Whew! I thought it might be a pink slip."

We laughed, but it showed me we needed to keep encouraging her and continue checking in. Over time, Laura got better and better at the role. She continued to grow and develop, and now she's excelling in her position. Debbie and I believed in her more than she believed in herself. We saw her potential and watched her step into it.

Laura's growth inside the company has been gratifying enough. But she stepped out of another box during this same period. For years, Laura volunteered for an organization dedicated to celebrating women who worked in factories during World War II (the actual Rosie the Riveters). Four years ago, she mostly helped them put together and mail out their newsletter, basically doing a data entry role for them too.

As Laura's confidence grew at work, she also started taking on more responsibilities in her volunteer role. She helped put on a national conference and was then offered a board role. Fast-forward to today: Laura is now the president of the organization, which was recently honored in Washington, DC, by receiving a Congressional Gold Medal by the United States Congress for their work.

We are so proud of Laura, and she's only one example of a team member who blossomed once we encouraged them to get out of their box. A huge part of our success over the last four years is directly related to how many members of our team—mostly the same people, just in new positions—have grown and developed.

How many "Lauras" are on your team? Let's find out. This chapter teaches a mindset shift you can easily make to transform the results you get from the people on your team. It's something I call making the Hero Assumption.

THE HERO ASSUMPTION

Quick quiz: When you get up in the morning and you're brushing your teeth and looking in the mirror, do you ever think to yourself, "I can't wait to get to work and screw up everything I touch"?

I didn't think so. Nobody does that. Nobody wakes up thinking they are the villain of their story; they are the hero.

You are the hero.

The Hero Assumption is all about the stories we tell ourselves. These stories are rooted in our beliefs, and our beliefs are shaped by what we perceive as possible. Stories are how we imagine both the possible and the impossible for ourselves and others.

To complete a heroic journey, heroes must believe in themselves. But they also need someone else to believe in them, someone who can keep the boat afloat when the dark times come and the doubt settles in.

Think back to the hero leader you chose at the end of the introduction (you did do your homework, right?). I bet you chose someone who believed in you. Often these leaders are people who believed in us during a time when we were unsure about ourselves. They encouraged us to try something that was a stretch or assume a role we would never have imagined for ourselves. They are able to see us two or three steps ahead of where we are on our journey.

These leaders also help us keep obstacles in perspective. When my friend Nate saw that I was stuck, he also saw and believed that I had what it takes to turn things around. He encouraged me to step into the role I'd need to fill in order to take my team to the next level.

There are two pillars that support the Hero Assumption. The first is the Pygmalion myth. This teaches us about how belief creates a self-fulfilling prophecy. The second is Joseph Campbell's mono-myth, the hero's journey. This reminds us about the stages of growth required to reach our fullest potential.

PILLAR ONE: THE PYGMALION MYTH

Pillar One is based on the Greek myth about a sculptor named Pygmalion. Pygmalion carved an ivory statue of a beautiful woman. As the woman's body began to appear beneath his hands, Pygmalion fell in love with her and even began to treat the sculpture as if it were a real woman. Desperately wishing the statue to come to life, Pygmalion sought out the goddess Aphrodite to grant his wish. Upon returning home from his visit to Aphrodite, Pygmalion kissed the statue and found that his wish had been granted—her lips were warm. The statue came to life, and Pygmalion married the woman he created from rock.

The Pygmalion myth is such a compelling story that it has been re-created in art over and over through the years. *Pinocchio* is a modern retelling. So is *My Fair Lady*, the musical and eventual movie featuring Audrey Hepburn, both of which were based on George Bernard Shaw's play *Pygmalion*. Each of these examples teaches us that we are the caretakers of our dreams. When you envision something you want so much that your prophecy is fulfilled, that's Pygmalion. The belief creates the behavior, and the behavior creates the result. You are the sculptor. You ultimately bring your dreams to life.

PILLAR TWO: THE HERO'S JOURNEY

Joseph Campbell, in his classic 1949 book *The Hero with a Thousand Faces*,[1] calls the hero's journey the monomyth: the underlying story for all civilizations and cultures in history. Every major religion and culture share this same mythical structure as a part of the core story that shapes their beliefs. There are three steps to the hero's journey: departure, initiation, and return.

DEPARTURE

The departure involves three parts. The first is the call to adventure. This is where somebody believes in the hero and calls the hero to begin the journey. Often this call is refused.

Next, the hero commits to the journey, usually spurred on by some sort of supernatural aid, which Christopher Vogler, a Disney screenwriter, describes as an event or person who influences the hero to believe they can complete the journey. The hero then leaves the known world and crosses the threshold into the unknown.

The last part of the departure is the negative event. Almost always, something bad happens early in the journey. Campbell calls it the "belly of the whale." The hero faces a big obstacle and questions whether they've made a major mistake. But here they also show a willingness to change and transform.

INITIATION

The next step of the journey is initiation. Initiation is a series of trials and obstacles that tests the hero. He meets enemies. He makes friends and people who offer help. He is tempted to leave the path but ultimately decides to complete the journey and is rewarded. He becomes the hero. But his journey is not yet complete.

RETURN

The final part of the hero's journey is the return. He returns home but as a different person. Often the hero is tempted to continue the adventure, which Campbell calls the refusal of the return.

Ultimately he does return home, crossing the threshold and becoming the master of two worlds. The hero then serves as an inspiration and mentor to those he left behind while on the journey.

Departure, initiation, and return—that's the hero's journey. And it all begins with the call from a mentor who believes in you and challenges you to go forth, to become the hero.

COMBINING THE TWO PILLARS

The Hero Assumption combines the two pillars: the hero's journey and the Pygmalion myth. While both pillars deal with transformation, on their own they each lack a key component for success in today's world.

In the hero's journey, the hero is often alone without the support of a mentor, the person who most likely encouraged the hero to go on the journey in the first place. The journey itself becomes lonely and is often treacherous. In stories, the hero presses on. But in the real world, obstacles and self-doubt keep many of us from completing the journeys we're called to make.

By contrast, the Pygmalion myth isn't always heroic—it simply describes a self-fulfilling prophecy. And there can also be a dark side to it. The prophecy can be negative, like with the nocebo effect. As Henry Ford said, "Whether you believe you will succeed or you will fail, you're right." If you believe you or someone around you is going to fail or is a failure, that belief can become self-fulfilling. This is what I call the Villain Assumption.

That's why the Hero Assumption is so important. It starts with a positive belief, a belief in the potential for greatness. The mentor believes the mentee is the hero of the story and can be, and wants to be, great. This belief turns into behavior that turns into transformation—thus, combining the hero's journey with the Pygmalion myth.

BECOMING BATMAN

"It's not what you look at that matters, it's what you see."
—HENRY DAVID THOREAU

I've always loved Batman. I liked that he was a detective who didn't have superpowers, so he had to develop his physical and intellectual abilities on his own. I admired him over other heroes whose powers came from being born on another planet or by some science experiment gone awry. Batman always seemed attainable to me, as though I had the potential to be him if I worked hard enough and really wanted to.

There actually is a real-life Batman. And he is more impressive than anything you'll see in the comic books. His name is Daniel Kish, and he is a remarkable human being.

One of my favorite pictures of Daniel captures him riding a mountain bike on a trail covered in water that comes up over his pedals. This is not easy terrain. It requires strength and experience to safely maneuver a mountain bike through running water.

One thing that's not immediately evident when looking at that picture is what makes Daniel so remarkable. Daniel is *completely blind*. He's been blind since birth. He was born with cancer in his eyes that required them to be removed at thirteen months old.

Despite being blind, Daniel learned to see with his other senses. He's so good at this that he can hike and mountain bike on uncertain terrain. He can sit down on a park bench and draw his surroundings. From the playground equipment to trees, and even other benches, Daniel can do this over and over again in parks he's never been to before. He does this through echolocation, by clicking his tongue and listening for the sound to reflect off objects in the area.[2] It's the same thing bats and dolphins use to "see" what they can't actually see. Daniel taught himself to do this. It's his superpower—and he's a real-life Batman.

HOW DANIEL KISH BECAME BATMAN

When most sighted individuals see Daniel show off his gift, they can't believe it's not a trick. That's because most sighted individuals don't make the Hero Assumption about the blind. They assume that people without sight can't be allowed to navigate on their own without hurting or even killing themselves.

They've never met Daniel Kish.

Daniel says that conventions are maintained only by our beliefs. Once he believed that he could navigate his way through the world using reflections of sound, he transformed himself into the first totally blind certified mobility specialist. Today he trains other blind people not only how to echolocate but also how to train others to do it. As Daniel says:

> What happens when we dare to fly against convention, changing our beliefs and challenging everything we think we know?[3]

With the help of Daniel's efforts and example, numerous research projects now show that people who are blind can redeploy their visual brain using echolocation, allowing them to truly see and appreciate the world around them. MRIs even show that when Daniel or someone he's trained clicks their tongue, the reflected sound they receive back lights up the same parts of the brain that trigger when a sighted person sees an object with their eyes.

THE REAL HEROES OF DANIEL'S STORY

Daniel Kish's ability to "see" through echolocation is an incredible story. But I don't think he's the only hero here. The true heroes are Daniel's parents.

Daniel developed his ability to click his tongue and then map in his brain what a sighted person might see with their eyes through trial and error. As a kid, Daniel's parents refused to treat him as a blind person. They encouraged him to engage in activities that most parents would think are crazy and irresponsible for a blind child. Other parents often feared he would get hurt or killed because his parents weren't paying enough attention to him—they weren't putting him in the same safety box most people believe a blind child belongs in.

Instead, Daniel's parents let him play on playground equipment with other kids. They let him walk on sidewalks and close to traffic. They refused to put him in a bubble the way almost all parents of blind children do. They gave Daniel space to explore and develop abilities that other blind people have but never get the chance to cultivate. And because of their deliberate decision, a miracle happened that changed the entire world for Daniel and ultimately impacted the lives of many, many other blind people.

Daniel founded a group that teaches this echolocation ability to blind children all over the world. His work raises a couple of important questions we should all be asking ourselves:

- What limiting beliefs do I have about myself today?
- What limiting beliefs do I have about others?

Once Daniel Kish's parents decided not to treat him as a blind kid, their behavior changed. That shift in their mind altered the way they engaged with him, which then changed Daniel's belief in himself. We rarely think about the things we just accept as true, but we should. Because once you accept something as true, you behave as if it is true. That behavior has ripple effects that may not be what you intend and could negatively impact you and the world around you.

SMART RATS VERSUS DUMB RATS—THE PYGMALION EFFECT

The Pygmalion myth is essentially a story about self-fulfilling prophecy. When you believe something is true, it becomes true. The research on the Pygmalion effect takes this classic myth and asks whether it plays out in the real world. Two definitive studies answer this question.

The preeminent researcher in the field of self-fulfilling prophecy (sometimes called expectancy theory) is Dr. Robert Rosenthal. One early study he conducted with Kermit L. Fode looked at lab rats going through mazes.[4]

The study was set up using numerous lab rats and unwitting

college psychology students. Researchers evenly divided out the normal lab rats, but then they told the students that some of them had "maze-bright" rats and others had "maze-dull" rats. The maze-bright rats were supposedly gifted at doing mazes, and the maze-dull rats were disadvantaged at mazes. Remember, there was no actual test to figure out which rat is the smartest or best at mazes.

Still, the researchers assigned the rats and had the students start running these rats through the mazes. The rats that belonged to students who believed their rats were maze-dull finished the mazes slower than the rats who were dubbed maze-bright.

This effect compounded over time. On the second day, students continued running the rats through the mazes. Both kinds of rats showed improvement on day two, but the supposedly maze-bright rats improved more than the maze-dull ones. By day three, the maze-dull rats stopped improving, while the maze-bright rats continued to increase their pace getting through the maze. Here are the results:

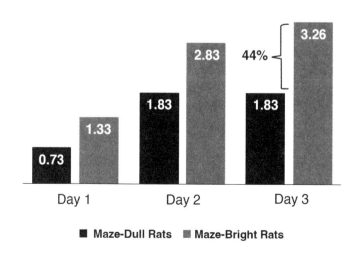

There was no physical or mental difference in the rats. The only difference was the belief the students had in their rats' ability to complete the maze. There are numerous explanations for the results of this study. The most compelling one is simple but powerful: the belief the students had in the maze-bright rats created an encouraging and exciting environment for maze running. This, in turn, resulted in more successful maze running.

Alternatively, the students with maze-dull rats expected their rats to perform poorly. So they had no confidence in the ability of their rats to run mazes, and they lacked the same encouragement and excitement that the so-called maze-bright rats enjoyed from their student cheering section. This also led to the expected result: poor maze running.

The researchers were able to repeat this result again and again. Astonishingly, if you simply change the belief the student observers have in the ability of their rats, it changes the performance of the rats in the real world.

ACADEMIC "BLOOMERS" STUDY

The Pygmalion effect study I find most compelling deals with the IQ of schoolchildren. It was conducted by Dr. Rosenthal and Dr. Lenore Jacobson.[5] In this study, teachers were told that some of their students were "academic bloomers," so they should expect these students to flourish substantially over the course of the year. The research question being analyzed was whether this expectation by the teachers would create a self-fulfilling prophecy and play out in the real world the same way it played out in the lab rat studies.

The study was done in poor school districts. The researchers examined the IQs of elementary school students and then tested their academic competence using a Harvard-developed assessment of verbal and math ability. Next, they divided the students into classrooms to create controlled conditions where students who shared similar IQ and ability scores were grouped together.

Then, like the college psychology students in the maze studies, the researchers played a trick on the teachers. They told the teachers that some students scored highly on the Harvard ability tests and were expected to "bloom" (have a significant jump in their IQs) over the course of the school year. The researchers randomly selected which students would be designated as bloomers because the ability test scores did not actually predict blooming. In fact, IQs tend to remain relatively stable by the time a child enters elementary school.[6]

I want to emphasize that this wasn't a situation where one class of students was labeled gifted while another was not. The bloomers were in classes with other students with similar IQs, but whom the teachers did not expect to thrive. All students were receiving the same instruction from the same teacher all year long.

The results of the study were as remarkable as the maze experiments and can be seen on the following page.

During that school year, the bloomers averaged 24.9 more academic IQ points than the non-bloomer control group students. Therefore, about half of the non-bloomer children saw their IQs improve by ten or more points. But among the bloomers, 79 percent went up more than ten points, and almost half went up more than twenty points. Astonishingly, 21 percent of the bloomers

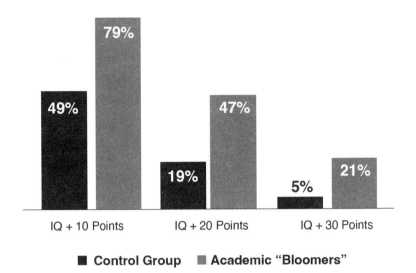

went up more than thirty points, compared to just 5 percent of the non-bloomers.

This was a remarkable difference in achievement. And the only reason for the change in real-world performance was the teachers' assumptions that these academic bloomers were going to bloom.

What happened in the classrooms that led to these extraordinary achievements? The behavior changes were subtle. For example, if a teacher was working with a student in the control group who was struggling with a concept, they might jump in to help, assuming the student would feel embarrassed to be having such a hard time in front of their peers.

But if that same teacher was dealing with a bloomer in an identical situation, they would push the student to work through the problem a bit longer—in this case, assuming that the struggle might be an opportunity for the child to bloom. That encouragement and confidence in the bloomer triggered a self-fulfilling prophecy—the student would solve the problem and improve.

The teachers behaved differently around the bloomers because they believed the bloomers were about to grow and the other students weren't.

THE TAKEAWAY

The Pygmalion research has incredibly important implications for leaders. Teachers are leaders in the classroom. And the Pygmalion research repeatedly proves that the belief the leader has in the ability of each teammate impacts the performance of that teammate. This is true even when the leader's belief is factually wrong. Whatever the leader believes changes what happens in the real world.

Leaders in companies, especially first-level or "frontline" leaders, often feel powerless. The Pygmalion research shows that the belief you have in others—whether you make the Hero Assumption or not—will become its own self-fulfilling prophecy. This is a far cry from being powerless. You are powerful beyond your imagination.

WHO BELIEVED IN YOU?

I got sent home from school with my share of notes to my mom, but I never faced the embarrassment Thomas Edison did when he was eight. The story, loosely based on fact, goes that Edison's teacher sent him home with a note pinned to his shirt. His instructions were to go straight home and have his mom read the note. Somehow, he resisted the urge to open it (or accidentally lose it).

Upon arriving home, his mom unpinned the note and started to read it. Tears began welling up in her eyes, and Edison asked, "Mama, what's wrong? What's it say?" She replied:

> Dear Mrs. Edison,
> Your son is a genius and our school is so small, we don't have appropriate teachers. Can you please educate him at home?

Mrs. Edison folded the note and put it away.

You know the rest of the story. Edison became a famous, wildly successful inventor who transformed the world . . . but that's not all of it.

Years later, Edison's mom died. While cleaning up her house, he ran across the yellowed letter, squirreled away in a box somewhere. He recognized it as soon as he saw it. He opened it up. To his shock, he found that the letter actually read:

> Dear Mrs. Edison,
> Your child is mentally deficient. We cannot have him in school. He is expelled.

Edison wrote in his diary that day that this was the moment his mom turned an imbecile into the genius of the century. But I think he's wrong about that. This wasn't the moment his mom turned him into a genius. This was the moment she made the Hero Assumption about him.

She knew he was a genius. She believed in him and understood what he was capable of. She also knew what was probably happening at school. Her son was bored and miles ahead of everybody else.

He wasn't a great rule follower. And these things surely made him disruptive at times.

Rather than noticing Edison's strengths and thinking outside the box about his challenging behavior, his teacher made the Villain Assumption about him. He saw a disruptive child who would not do his work. Where the teacher saw a lack of intelligence, Mrs. Edison saw genius.

Edison had all kinds of failures and massive setbacks on his way to becoming one of the world's greatest inventors. But he also had unwavering faith and belief in himself. Being smart is great, but you don't succeed because you're smart. You succeed because you believe in your ability to put that intellect to work. And usually, you believe in yourself that much because someone else believed in you first. At least, that was the case for Edison.

You have that same potential for everyone you lead. Just like your own hero leader, your belief in your teammate may be the spark they need to get past an obstacle or reach that next goal. And that starts with a belief in yourself.

To paraphrase Henry Ford, whether you think someone on your team can do something or they can't, you'll be right. As a leader, your assumptions about your team directly impact how they perform in the real world. Sound impossible? Study after study proves it is true.

The Hero Assumption combines the hero's journey with the Pygmalion myth. If you believe somebody is the hero of the story, if you believe they want to be great, your belief can be just like Pygmalion asking Aphrodite to make his statue real. Your belief makes it happen.

But it all starts with a belief in yourself. You have to believe that you have the influence and the power to inspire and lead your teammates on their own hero's journey. This is so powerful because our belief affects our behavior. It's not enough to just say, "You got this; I know you're great." You must also act like you believe. Celebrate when your mentee reaches a milestone. Coach them when they fall short of an expectation. Be available when they have a decision to make. And above all else, never lose faith.

ASSUME POSITIVE INTENT

Have you ever heard of Hanlon's Razor? It's a mental model or rule of thumb used in science and philosophy. The most common version states: "Never attribute to malice that which is adequately explained by stupidity." It teaches the very important principle that bad intentions are rarely the correct explanation for behavior you don't like.

The common version of Hanlon's Razor isn't exactly making the Hero Assumption. My favorite version of the rule, which I learned from my friend Austin Clary, is this: "Always assume positive intent."

If somebody does something you think is dumb, or they perform in a way that disappoints you, assume positive intent. What they said was due to inexperience or lack of knowledge. The disappointing performance didn't turn out the way they planned. They meant the best, and it just didn't work out this time.

This mental model is a great way (the fancy word is a *heuristic*) to force your brain to default to the Hero Assumption.

RETURNING TO YOUR EVERYDAY HERO

"I've sat through this exercise probably a dozen times, and I always think of the same leader. But I've never reached out to him," an HR leader blurted out in one of our workshops.

In one workshop we do an exercise called "everyday leader" where we ask participants to describe an influential leader in their lives and later challenge them to reach out to that leader and thank them. (You've done that already, right?) One of our Fortune 100 manufacturing clients held a lot of workshops, and their HR leaders would rotate through classes to introduce us and help with logistics. Because of this, they'd participate in numerous workshops.

During one workshop, an HR leader named Courtney spoke up during the exercise. "Hey, everyone, I really want to encourage you to reach out to your leader. Let me tell you what happened to me when I did it." She had everyone's attention, including mine. Courtney continued her story:

"He was the first person who really believed in me and encouraged me to try for a leadership position. The last time I attended the workshop, I decided I was actually going to do it. So after the workshop, I called him. It had been a long time since we last talked, and he was in a new role. Honestly, I felt pretty awkward calling him, which I guess is why I put it off. I told him I had been in this leadership class and we were asked to think about someone who was influential in our lives, and I thought of him."

Courtney started getting emotional at this point. "Then everything went silent. I thought maybe the call had dropped. I asked if he was still there, and he choked out, 'Yeah, I'm here; give me a second.' I realized he was crying. After a bit he said, 'Courtney, I don't know what made you decide to make this call right now, but you have no idea how important it was for me to hear that today.' Eventually we were able to catch up, and he said several times how grateful he was to hear from me and to hear how he'd impacted my life. I was *so* glad I made that call."

Here's a text another workshop attendee forwarded me. She reached out to her leader during a break in one of our training sessions:

As a leader, you impact your team every day, and you usually have no idea when it's happening. These are the ripples you leave in the lives of your team members every single day. Maybe you'll be lucky like Courtney's or Brenda's old boss and have someone tell you what you've meant in their life. My hope for you is that one day you get that call. But either way, know that you ARE having an impact.

But there's a problem: every leader isn't like Courtney's or Brenda's everyday leader. And since it's not always obvious the impact you're having, your ripples could be more like tidal waves.

LEADING PEOPLE THROUGH THE HERO ASSUMPTION

As we think about ourselves as mentors or leaders, how can we help those we lead get through these times of doubt? Laura wasn't sure she had what it took when we changed her role. Daniel surely had moments of doubt as he learned to navigate the world without sight. What can we do to guide them out of Campbell's "belly of the whale"? As we learned in the previous chapter, it all starts with our belief in ourselves.

You must believe that your words and actions matter—that you are making an impact, especially on those days when it doesn't seem like you are. Take a little time thinking about the impact you've already made on your teammates. Who have you already inspired to grow and to thrive?

This belief in yourself drives your belief in your teammates. That in turn drives your actions. When your actions are consistent with your beliefs, then your behavior—both encouragement and occasionally disappointment—reinforces to the hero that you believe they are the hero. Ultimately, they begin to believe that about themselves, and the journey is complete.

MOVING PAST THE PHONINESS (AND REALLY CONNECTING)

*"To handle yourself, use your head; to
handle others, use your heart."*
—Eleanor Roosevelt

"**I** work with this guy Tom, and we've *hated* each other for seventeen years. How would *you* deal with *that*?" Gulp. A quality supervisor named Kim asked me this after I delivered one of our workshops in a pipe plant in Ohio.[1] And I had no idea how to respond.

"Seventeen years?" I stammered. "How is that possible?" Kim went on to tell me that she had a quality position, and Tom worked in a department she oversaw. Each week she had to go over quality numbers with him, and it was excruciating every time she had to do it. Over the years they had basically trained themselves to make the Villain Assumption about each other.

After a little discussion, I told her, "Look, here's the bad news. There isn't some kind of magic dust you sprinkle that solves all your problems. But let's come up with a plan and see if it helps."

Our plan was for Kim to start by stating the obvious: these two couldn't stand each other, and this weekly meeting was stressful and terrible for them both. After sharing how she felt about him and the meeting, and empathizing that Tom must share some of these same feelings about her, we then decided to ask a version of one of the questions we teach in the workshop: What would make work better?

"Point to the form you have to fill out and ask Tom for advice about what could make that form better," I suggested. "Then see what he has to say. It can't be any worse than what you've been dealing with for the last seventeen years."

Kim came in after the last workshop the next day to report on the conversation. I held my breath—like I said, this stuff isn't magic.

"I can't believe it," she said, "but it was like I was talking to a different person."

"Really?" I said, trying not to act surprised. "What happened?"

"As soon as I pointed to the form and asked him what would make it better, Tom started smiling and made a couple of suggestions." Speaking of different people, Kim was brimming with confidence. "These were easy changes, so I agreed to fix them. Then we had the first normal conversation we'd had in seventeen years. I don't know if this is going to last, but it really worked."

A year later, we were back in that plant training another group of supervisors. I can't report that Kim and Tom are hosting each other's families for game nights or anything, but Kim said that every conversation they'd had after that was fine.

Just like Kim and Tom, every hero must overcome obstacles as part of their journey. You'll face obstacles with your team too. This last set of tools will help you overcome them. Not every situation will work out as well as Kim and Tom's did, but you'll be surprised at how many bad relationships can turn around with the right approach.

THE FLYING PEN AND MAKING *REAL* CONNECTIONS

In our company, I know we are really connecting when a pen flies during our leadership team meeting. The pen is normally thrown by Debbie, and she throws it at whoever made her cry.

I know what you're thinking: *People cry in your company meetings? Are you talking about* before *you turned things around?* Nope. My team may have been crying before (we've already established I wasn't paying close attention then), but if they were, it was behind closed doors. Today we cry out in the open.

Before you get the wrong impression, we're not walking around the office blubbering all the time. And these aren't usually sad tears. It's not uncommon for our team to share genuine, heartfelt thanks with one another or celebrate a milestone together. That sometimes leads to tears of joy—which is awesome.

Since starting our transformation four years ago, we had a *lot* of work to do to build our culture and our team, starting with my relationship with the leadership team. Once I recognized the dysfunction I was causing, I knew I needed help to renew and repair relationships, starting with Debbie. This required some serious conversations, and it required me to be vulnerable.

I quickly realized that the biggest cause of our issues was that, even though we'd worked in the same small company for over a decade, Debbie and I really didn't know each other that well. And we both got on each other's nerves.

As I mentioned in "The 1st Shift," the turning point between Debbie and me was when we read *Rocket Fuel*. It decoded the fact that someone like me is custom-built to drive someone like Debbie crazy. It explained a lot about the frustrations we experienced with each other over the years. It also explained how tension like this is *necessary* to make a company like ours successful.

We had some frank, no-holds-barred discussions about how we would work together. It was the first time in the nearly fifteen years we'd known each other that we'd ever talked about our work relationship. Debbie was surprised at my willingness to hand over control of a lot of the day-to-day to her—which is ironic because I hate that stuff (and am terrible at it). I think she was also surprised that I was willing to be so vulnerable about what I saw as my shortcomings, and how I saw that I was holding the organization (and her) back.

At the same time, she acknowledged what I bring to the company and saw how reorganizing things could really free me up to do the things I am uniquely suited to do and that generate the most value. Things that used to drive her crazy she saw in an entirely new light. I began to appreciate things about her that used to annoy me before. We quickly saw how this new partnership could transform our culture and our company.

Once we established that foundation, the next step was to build relationships with the rest of the team, starting with the leadership team. It was during these meetings that the pen-throwing started. For us to overcome our past challenges and really become a strong leadership team, we had to trust one another. Trust requires vulnerability, and vulnerability sometimes comes with some tears.

When I cry, I just do the whole "ugly cry" thing. But when Debbie cries, she throws things like pens. (Although I think she threw a Kleenex box once, and we now try to keep heavy objects away from her during meetings.)

COMPANIES PERFORM BETTER WHEN THEY INVEST IN RELATIONSHIPS

I know that most readers of this book don't own a company and aren't in a position to snap their fingers and change their company's (or maybe even their department's) structure or strategy. But I hope you recognize that the changes we made to our culture had *nothing* to do with the strategy process we implemented, or because I was the one pushing them.

Our success had *everything* to do with our relationships. We were willing to be vulnerable with one another and build trust first. The spark that turned around our culture was the fact that we invested first in building stronger relationships. The results came from the relationships.

In 2012, Google decided to ask a really important question:

"Why do some Google teams shine while others stumble?" When you happen to be Google, you have access to some of the smartest statisticians, organizational psychologists, sociologists, and engineers around. Google deployed this incredible talent on a quest to find out what makes their best teams click. They dubbed the assignment Project Aristotle.[2]

Project Aristotle researchers looked at teams in every possible way to figure out what set apart the teams that excelled at Google versus the teams that didn't. Some of the correlations they looked at included:

- Were the teams made up of people with similar interests?
- Were they motivated by the same kind of rewards?
- Did teammates socialize outside the office? How often?
- How did their education backgrounds compare to one another?
- Were teammates outgoing or shy?
- What was the gender ratio of each team?

DO PERSONALITY TYPES, SKILLS, OR BACKGROUNDS PREDICT TEAM SUCCESS? NO.

Over the course of a year, the researchers looked at 180 teams from all over the company and found no patterns showing that a particular combination of skills or personality types could determine the success of the group. Each time they thought they had narrowed down a set of group norms (the rules and expectations that govern how team members behave and interact), they would discover another, equally successful team with the complete opposite set of characteristics.

As time went on, however, the researchers recognized two behaviors that all good teams shared:

- First, all members spoke for approximately the same amount of time, a practice known as conversational turn-taking. The collective intelligence of the group would decline unless everyone had an opportunity to speak and no one person or small group of people dominated the conversation.

- Second, good teams all had high "average social sensitivity," meaning they were skilled at understanding how others felt based on their tone of voice, expressions, and other nonverbal cues.

Coincidentally (or not), conversational turn-taking and average social sensitivity are traits of psychological safety. Harvard Business School professor Amy Edmondson defines *psychological safety* as:

> a shared belief held by members of a team that the team is safe for interpersonal risk-taking. . . . [It instills] a sense of confidence that the team will not embarrass, reject, or punish someone for speaking up. . . . It describes a team climate characterized by interpersonal trust and mutual respect in which people are comfortable being themselves.[3]

Project Aristotle researchers found that while there were many behaviors that seemed important to establish as team norms, psychological safety was the most critical. That begged the question . . .

HOW DO YOU ESTABLISH PSYCHOLOGICAL SAFETY?

Sure, you can tell people to do things like listen more, take turns talking, or pay more attention to people's feelings and notice when they're upset, but does that really ever work? Most of the time it just goes in one ear and out the other. After all, who wants to be reminded of proper social decorum?

These changes tend to develop organically. But someone has to plant the seed. And that responsibility falls on the leader. That's what Project Aristotle found. And I agree.

One manager at Google, when confronted with the Project Aristotle research, realized that his team didn't clearly understand their role in the overall goal of the company, nor did they think the work they did had much of an impact.

This bothered the manager so much that he gathered the group off-site to try to get to the bottom of where these feelings came from. Once he had them all there, he suddenly felt moved to share with them that he'd been battling cancer. For the first time, he allowed himself to be vulnerable to his team.

The next thing he knew, someone else shared something they'd been dealing with in their personal life. Then someone else shared. It continued on and on this way. It was like these people, who saw and spoke with one another every day, finally felt comfortable being vulnerable with one another for the first time. According to the *New York Times*, one member said:

> [U]ntil the off-site, I had separated things in my head into work life and life life. . . . But the thing is, my work is my life. I spend the majority of my time working.

Most of my friends I know through work. If I can't be open and honest at work, then I'm not really living, am I?[4]

There is an undeniable link between the way people feel about work and the quality of work they produce. Leading begins with connection. And your culture is only as strong as your connections.

This Google manager learned that it was up to him to take the first steps to create a psychologically safe environment—one in which people feel comfortable speaking up when they have ideas. One in which they feel safe to share what's going on in their work and personal lives, both good and bad. One in which relationships are strong and collaboration is constant.

GOOD THINGS EMAILS

One of the best things we did for our culture was what Debbie calls her "Good Things" emails. A Good Things email is sent whenever Debbie wants to tell the team about something good happening with her or someone else on the team. She sends one about once a week, and over the last four years, we've challenged everyone on the leadership team to send them.

These emails are sometimes funny, sometimes sad, and always vulnerable ("I'm not crying; you're crying!"). They are a regular reminder from someone at the very top of the company that it's OK to be vulnerable and tell people how you're feeling—whether that's great or not so great. And these emails often will start a conversation among the team.

Leaders, being vulnerable with your team is a critical component to building psychological safety. Wait! Don't shut the book, thinking I'm about to ask you to hold hands in a circle and share your deepest, darkest secrets. You don't have to share things that might make you or your team uncomfortable (that can reduce psychological safety). But you should work hard to create a culture in which teammates are willing to be vulnerable with one another. You should build that into your team meetings (stay tuned for some examples of how to do that below). And there is no way this will happen if the leader isn't sharing themselves and setting the stage for others to do so.

HOW TO AVOID BEING A CHEW TOY FOR A SABER-TOOTHED TIGER

Are you the kind of person who cares what people think about you? It would be weird if you weren't. That's because we are genetically hardwired to want acceptance from others.

Back when our ancestors were running from woolly mammoths and saber-toothed tigers, acceptance wasn't just trying to feel good about ourselves. Getting excluded from the group was a death sentence. The worst punishment in those times was getting shunned from the tribe.

Because of this, we humans developed a strong capacity for cooperation and social connection. A huge part of that capability lies in our ability to read and interpret the (primarily nonverbal) signals from others and adjust our behavior to gain acceptance.

Some argue (and I agree) that we have taken this need for acceptance way too far. But there's no question that these skills serve us

QUESTION THREE: DO YOU THINK I'M WORTH THE EFFORT?

Things aren't always going to go right. We screw up. Despite our best efforts, we all have days when we take a few steps back. These are times when even the most self-accepting person gets on shaky ground.

How do you act toward your team when things are in the ditch? Do you show up with encouragement and support or do you give up on them? Now we're back to value and self-worth: Do you think I'm worth the effort?

Think about that question for a moment and how it might affect someone. How does it affect you?

True leadership is about so much more than making sure the work gets handled. Yes, that's technically your job. And you have to make sure your job gets done. But when you step into the role of a leader, something else happens. Your opinion begins to matter on a deeper level.

You're going to have to deal with those inevitable situations when things are going a little sideways, such as negative performance discussions and dealing with conflicts. But remember, underneath all these conversations, your teammates want to know the answers to those three questions:

1. Do you like me?
2. Do you think I have what it takes?
3. Do you think I'm worth the effort?

Even when the conversation is difficult, make sure every conversation you have leaves them feeling like the answers to those questions are: Yes, yes, and yes!

YOUR TURN: YOUR ACCEPTANCE TOOLKIT

Before we get into dealing with coaching employees who are facing challenges on their hero's journey, let's make sure you can answer the three acceptance questions.

You could just come out and say, "I like you," or "I think you have what it takes," or "I think you're worth the effort." And if someone were to ask you the questions directly, those are probably the right things to say. But remember, these questions are almost never asked directly. If you randomly blurt out one of these answers, you might make your teammate more anxious, or even weird them out. Either way, not good.

Most of the time you'll want to communicate the answers to the three acceptance questions subtly. Here are some suggestions for different ways you can get across the same idea, but then you should brainstorm some phrases in your own words to help build out your tool kit.

"I Like You" Phrases
I really enjoy working with you.
You are fun to work with.
I really admire the energy you bring to the team.
I always appreciate the chance to work with you.
Being around you just makes my day better.

"I Think You Have What It Takes" Phrases
You got this!
You really do a great job.
Your work is always stellar.
I really admire your skill and talent.
You may not notice, but we all admire your work.

"I Think You're Worth the Effort" Phrases
I look forward to seeing how far you go with this.
It's great to coach you— I can see you're going to run with this.
This is tough, but I'm glad we're working on it together.
Pressure is how diamonds get made, and you're a diamond.
We're going to look back at this and laugh one day.

OTHER WAYS YOU CAN CREATE PSYCHOLOGICAL SAFETY

BANISH YOUR INNER "KNOW-IT-ALL"

A lot of leaders feel like they need to know everything about their area—they consider not knowing a sign of weakness. And new or inexperienced leaders often feel self-conscious about asking for advice. They fear others may not respect them if they don't know it all. This inner "Know-It-All" kills a team culture and often destroys the leader who is hoping to succeed.

If this is an area you need work in—and it is for many leaders—I highly recommend Edgar Schein's book *Humble Inquiry*. Schein offers several practical tips, including the observation, "Telling puts the other person down. It implies the other person does not know what I am telling and that the other person ought to know it."[6]

Newer leaders should keep in mind Mark Twain's advice, "It's better to keep your mouth shut and appear stupid than open it and remove all doubt." If you're not actually an expert (and remember the Dunning-Kruger effect—if you think you're an expert, you could easily be wrong), then acting on your poor knowledge without advice from others just proves it. Now everyone thinks you're not up to the task.

Sure, some might say, "Why is she asking me when she's the boss?" (But are they really saying that, or are you just making the Villain Assumption?) Asking for advice in this situation shows self-confidence, helps speed up your learning curve, and builds bonds with your team. Remember, being a great leader isn't about how much you know but about how much you connect.

ASK FOR ADVICE

Once you are an expert, asking for advice becomes even more important (and valuable). When others see you as the expert, they are less likely to suggest things—they don't want you to judge their lack of knowledge or inexperience. The flip side is that when a true expert asks for advice, the person they are asking is truly honored.

Schein calls this "Here-and-Now Humility." When an expert asks for advice, they flip the power dynamic. The person in the higher-power position becomes dependent on the other person and thus, inferior. Schein suggests that you embrace this dynamic as often as possible. If a true expert wants to know what you think, you start to see yourself as the hero. And that's what we're going for.

Asking for advice even works when you are trying to repair a damaged relationship. In his autobiography, Benjamin Franklin tells a story about a new Pennsylvania Assembly member who gave a speech opposing Franklin in the Assembly.[7] Franklin did not understand why this man opposed him but realized he would be a very influential member. He needed to figure out a way to win him over.

Franklin decided the right approach wasn't to try to woo him or bow down to him. Instead, he used another approach. Franklin heard that this man had a "very scarce and curious book" in his library, and he wrote a note asking to borrow the book for a few days. The man sent it immediately. After a week, Franklin returned the book with a note thanking him for the favor.

The next time Franklin met the man in the House, he walked up to Franklin and warmly greeted him (he had never greeted Franklin before). Not only that, but he helped Franklin anytime he was asked, and they became great friends until the man died. Franklin explains that this is another proof of the old maxim, "He that has once done you a kindness will be more ready to do you another than he whom you yourself have obliged."

Not only does asking for advice make your coworker admire you for your good "judgment and wisdom," but by regularly seeking their opinion and advice, you are communicating that you value their opinion and that they have important things to contribute.

In one of our workshops, we ask participants to try Franklin's "ask for advice" approach. After attending the workshop, one participant we'll call Jeff later shared how he'd used this move successfully to repair a damaged relationship. When he first got into his position, he challenged one of the in-house attorneys at his company, one of the largest grocery retailers in the United States. He was young and trying to make his mark, but he realized later he had been rash and regretted his mistake. He could tell that the attorney held a grudge and that the relationship was damaged.

During our workshop Jeff committed to reaching out to the attorney. He originally proposed just talking to the attorney about the situation and hopefully repairing the damage. But I reminded Jeff that wasn't Franklin's approach—in fact, Franklin tried that same thing, and it didn't work. Instead, I asked him to think of some things the attorney knew a lot about—ideally something that wasn't work-related at all. Jeff remembered that the attorney was a big history buff, and Jeff was planning a trip with his family to Washington, DC. He decided to ask the attorney about suggestions for the trip. Later Jeff reported:

> I was pretty concerned about approaching him. He'd been frosty with me for years, and I could tell he was a little surprised I was there. But I told him about the trip and that I'd heard he was big into history. As soon as we started talking about historical sights, his whole demeanor changed. He warmed up, and by the end we were even joking with each other. The trip was a big success. We took a selfie in front of a Smithsonian exhibit he suggested and sent it to him on the trip. I later followed up to thank him for the advice and told him how much my kids enjoyed the sights he suggested. After that, our relationship was back on track. He's for sure the first person I'd approach in the legal department now.

YOUR TURN: ASK FOR ADVICE PART II

"Nobody ever listened his way out of a job."
—CALVIN COOLIDGE

In *The Approachability Playbook* I describe the problem of "power distance." This is the gap someone in a low-power position feels toward someone in a high-power position. In many relationships (like between a teacher and a student, a doctor and a patient, or a boss and her direct reports) the person in the low-power position often defers to the person in the higher-power position.

Low Power Distance
Relationship Focused

High Power Distance
Position/Authority Focused

Power distance can be high, low, or somewhere in between. When power distance is high, a lot of negative things happen. People hide or are afraid to share important information because they are worried about getting in trouble. Teams with high power distance often experience low productivity, quality problems, resistance to change, and even disastrous safety outcomes.

When relationships are strong, power distance is low. People feel much more comfortable being vulnerable and sharing with one another. Communication flows more freely. Teams characterized by low power distance are more productive, experience more organizational citizenship, are more engaged, and have lower turnover.

As you now know, a good way to flip the power relationship is to ask for advice. This naturally shrinks power distance. Daniel Coyle shares another great example of how to do this in his book *The Culture Playbook*.[8] He tells about an idea from Laszlo Bock, former CHRO of Google, called the Three-Line Email.

While Bock sent an email, I prefer using the same three lines in face-to-face conversations with individuals on my team. I use these each quarter when I hold my 1:1 conversation with my team (what we call our 5-5-5 quarterly conversations). Here are the questions:

1. What is one thing I currently do that you'd like me to continue to do?

2. What is one thing that I don't currently do frequently enough that you think I should do more often?

3. What can I do to make you more effective?

These questions make a great agenda for a 1:1 meeting. Asking for advice about how you can better support your teammate is a great way to shrink power distance.

COACHING SCRIPT: "WHAT'S WORKING? WHAT CAN WE DO BETTER?"

We don't do performance reviews at my company. Instead, we do quarterly conversations called 5-5-5 meetings.[9] A 5-5-5 meeting is a sit-down between each leader and the individuals they lead. The meeting takes around an hour, and we usually do them away from the office (a local coffee shop is a popular location for us).

The agenda for that meeting is simple. The leader and the team-mate look back at the last quarter and answer the questions "What's working?" and "What can we do better?" around three areas: core values, role, and rocks. The way we do it (which I adapted for our own culture) is that each person gives feedback on each topic.

For example, when I meet with someone, I first share with them examples of when I think they lived out our core values over the last quarter. Then I share any ideas I have for things they should continue to work on over the next quarter. Because we hire based on core values, it's rare that anyone is struggling with a core value (so much so that I changed the second question to "What can we do better?" instead of "What's not working?" because most of the time things are working!).

Next, I ask my teammate to tell me how they think I'm doing around the area of core values, and if there's anything they think I can do better. This may sound intimidating, and you may feel like your employees won't give you straight feedback. But remember what we said about psychological safety and asking for advice. I regularly get good feedback about things I should be working on as a leader to make the team more successful.

Once we discuss core values, we move on to roles ("What about your role is working, and what could be better?"). Again, both the leader and the employee give and receive feedback about their role. Finally, we shift to rocks, which means the major goals for the quarter, which are often refined by the "What can we do better?" items discussed earlier.

This process has been invaluable for our team. It ensures that each person—leader and non-leader—receives regular feedback about their value to the team, how they're doing, and what they can work on.

I don't think the 5-5-5 process is magic (and like I said, I modified it for my own team). However, you can ask these questions anytime you want, and I do think having a regular conversation (especially one that is two-way, in which you get feedback about what you can do better as well) is really important to building strong relationships with your team.

QUIET QUITTING AND HOW TO CATCH IT EARLY

There's a crisis around engagement. In a 2023 Gallup poll, 16 percent of employees said they are "actively disengaged."[10] They're not just unhappy at work; they're literally disruptive. They are complaining to coworkers and to management. They're intentionally not doing their job. In some cases, the actively disengaged try to sabotage the efforts of others.

In addition to nearly 20 percent of the workforce defining themselves as actively disengaged, the ratio of engaged employees to actively disengaged is 2.1 to 1. This is nearly the lowest this ratio has been in more than a decade. There just aren't very many people happy and engaged at work compared to those who are vocally negative. This creates a terrible work culture.

Active disengagement doesn't just create a bad culture. It also creates bad results. And it costs money . . . lots of money. In 2023, the estimated cost of disengagement globally was $8.8 trillion—per year.[11]

Further, huge numbers of workers are unhappy enough at their job to consider leaving in the next three to six months. The 16 percent that are actively disengaged are probably looking for work elsewhere. But Gallup estimates that 50 percent or more of these employees characterize themselves as quiet quitters.[12] They're rejecting the "hustle culture." They don't really see a point in going above and beyond at work.

They're quitting in place. This is the challenge that workplaces are facing every day today. Individual leaders are the linchpin to a lot of this labor market turmoil. Turnover, retention, and attracting new talent are all dependent on first-level leaders. And here's the problem: leaders are as frustrated and disengaged as their line-level employees.

That's one of the main points of this book. Companies have a lot of work to do to help build up leaders—to give them the skills and resources they need to be successful, while at the same time helping them attract and retain the new talent being brought in. The companies that do a good job of this are the ones that are going to see growth and stability.

If you know that people are quitting in droves, then the key next step is to figure out how to prevent someone from leaving. A lot of times leaders throw up their hands and say, "Well, you know, the labor market is churning. People are hearing all over the place about how they can get a better job, or they see signs for help all over town. What can I do to try to prevent someone from leaving?"

We've developed a practical tool you can use to recognize a "pre-quitter" before they actually quit. This gives you some strategies to re-recruit that person to continue to work for you—or to create a situation that makes the person think, *Wait a minute, I think this is actually a better opportunity than what else is out there.*

This Quiet Quit Early Warning System is based on research that was done at Utah State and later at Vanderbilt.[13] This research identified that there are thirteen signals, like a poker tell, that happen around ninety days before someone actually walks out the door. These thirteen signals can tell you if someone is considering leaving your organization.

This research is based on the commonsense idea that once your time horizon starts to shrink at work, your behavior changes. And it changes in three distinct categories.

The first one is your work performance. It drops. If you're not going to be here for your next performance appraisal, then you really don't care that much about impressing your boss or about getting a 10/10 on your review.

The second area is relationships. If you're leaving soon, then being on good terms with your manager doesn't matter much. And you also don't have to be nice to that person who annoys you just to try to keep things smooth at work. You're not even going to be here. You don't care.

And the third category is belonging. It's about how connected you feel to the organization and to your team. As the time horizon to your quiet quit shrinks, you spend way less time caring about these things. Why would you volunteer for the company event or engage in the company celebration when you're in the process of deciding whether you're even going to work there in the future?

YOUR TURN: THE QUIET QUIT TOOL AND CONNECTION CONVERSATIONS

Go through the Quiet Quit Tool with a list of your teammates and start thinking about these different work behaviors (you can download a full-size example of these tools at YourLeaderShift.com).

As you go through each section, ask whether this individual's work performance increased, decreased, or stayed about the same. Are they more or less involved in team activities? Does it seem like, behaviorally, their time horizon has shrunk? And so on.

This will give you an inventory of each person and whether they might be thinking about leaving. You'll also get a pretty good idea of how you might "re-recruit" that person if they are on their way out the door. We call this a Connection Conversation. During this conversation, you try to understand what is going on in your teammate's life, remind them of how valuable they are to the team, and get them reconnected. Hopefully they'll realize they really do have a good thing and now's not the time to leave.

There are four parts to the Connection Conversation. Part One is "Check In," when you ask permission to discuss what you're seeing. The easiest way to do this is to ask: "Do you mind if I check a story I've been telling myself?" This helps reduce power distance since you're asking for advice.

Part Two is "I Noticed." You describe one or two behaviors you noticed as you went through the Quiet Quit Tool. Even if you've noticed numerous signs of disconnection, you really only need to pick one or two for the conversation. For example, you might say, "I notice you didn't volunteer for the road cleanup—that used to be one of the things you led, and you take so much pride

Quiet-Quit Early Warning Signs

What Challenge Do I Face? — Which Tool Should I Use?	Performance	Relationship	Belonging
Work productivity decreased	✓		
Acting less like a team player			✓
Doing the minimum amount of work	✓		
Less interested in pleasing their manager		✓	
Less willing to commit to long-term timelines			✓
Exhibiting a negative change in attitude		✓	
Less effort and work motivation	✓		
Less focus on job-related matters	✓		
Expressing dissatisfaction with their current job	✓		
Expressing dissatisfaction with their supervisor		✓	
Leaving early from work			✓
Lost enthusiasm for the company			✓
Less interest in working with customers		✓	

in the neighborhood. The story I'm telling myself is that you're not feeling as connected to the team as you used to be. Do I have that right?" Once the conversation gets going, there will be an opportunity to discuss anything that's causing disconnection.

Part Three of the Connection Conversation is "I Appreciate." Here you reaffirm all the things the person brings to the team. Be specific about what you appreciate about them, and remember the three acceptance questions we learned earlier (Do you like me? Do you think I have what it takes? Do you think I'm worth the effort?).

Part Four is "Ask for Advice." Remember that asking for advice reduces power distance and creates psychological safety. For example, you might ask, "Is there anything you can think of that I could do to help you feel more connected?" Let your teammate help you understand what could re-attract them to the team. These conversations can stop quiet quitting in its tracks and reengage your actively disengaged employees. They are some of the most important conversations you can have as a leader.

YOUR TURN: BEST AND BEST

This is another way to make building strong relationships a part of your everyday meetings. This one is recommended by Gino Wickman in his book *Traction*.[14] Most meetings with my team begin with a round of "best and best" shares. Each person shares the best thing going on in their personal life and the best thing going on in their work life.

Personal shares are a great way to get to know one another better. They often give us a chance to celebrate together. But sometimes they help us identify an issue outside of work that is impacting someone on the team. Personal shares build understanding and closeness.

Work shares also help us celebrate something that otherwise might fly under the radar. It lets each person "show off" a little of their work to the team, and it keeps us updated as to what everyone is working on. Sometimes it also highlights where someone on the team might need some help. It's another great way to reinforce connections.

Try a round of Best and Best at your next team meeting. It's a really simple way to build relationships. It's been one of the key building blocks of our cultural transformation over the last four years.

YOUR TURN: ARON'S CLOSENESS QUESTIONNAIRE

WARNING: This next play is a proven way to create interpersonal closeness. It has even been known to lead to people falling in love![15]

Psychologist Arthur Aron and his wife, Elaine, spent much of their careers studying how humans grow feelings of closeness and whether there is a repeatable way to generate close interpersonal relationships. In the 1980s they developed an inventory of thirty-six questions that reliably increased closeness.[16]

The study found that strangers who go through the inventory are significantly closer afterward than a control group of strangers who engage in small talk instead. The magic of these questions is the way they progress. There are three question sets. The initial questions are low risk and low intensity. The second question set increases the level of personal disclosure, while the third set encourages sharing even deeper and more personal stories.

In *The Approachability Playbook* and in our workshops, we teach the Approachability Window (based on the Johari Window[17]), which offers a healthy way to grow relationships. There are two keys to that approach. First, increase vulnerability over time by sharing from your "hidden area" and asking for feedback on your "blind spot" area. Second, make people comfortable sharing by using the "offer-acceptance" approach. Here you make an "offer" by sharing first, and then you don't continue sharing until the other person "accepts" your offer by sharing something about themselves.

The Aron Closeness Questionnaire (ARQ) follows this same approach. Sharing is symmetrical (one person shares, followed by the other person sharing), building "offer" and "acceptance" into every conversation. You begin with shares that require little vulnerability and increase over time to shares that require more vulnerability.

As a leader at work, your goal isn't necessarily to have deep, intimate personal relationships with your team. However, your goal should be for people to feel comfortable sharing vulnerably with you. And that only happens when you have shown you are comfortable sharing vulnerably with them.

You won't sit down with each team member and go through all thirty-six questions on the ARQ. Instead, think of the ARQ as a resource list of conversation starters with your team. These make great icebreaker questions for the beginning of team meetings. They can also be great questions at the beginning of a 1:1 meeting with a team member. If a question seems too personal, don't ask it—or modify it to something you do feel comfortable asking.

You can download the thirty-six questions in the ARQ at YourLeaderShift.com. This is a terrific resource for building strong connections with your team.

THE TAKEAWAY

I hope you'll return to this chapter again and again. The foundation of any strong culture is the relationships between team members. We consider strengthening relationships our superpower, and I end this chapter by summarizing some of my favorite tools for making relationships strong. These are the same "plays" we've used to transform our own culture, including when to use them:

- Good Things (to celebrate the everyday events that make a culture great)

- Asking for Advice (to reduce power distance and create psychological safety)

- The Acceptance Toolkit (to answer the three questions your team wants to know but won't ask)

- What's Working? and What Can Be Better? (to encourage feedback)

- The Quiet Quit Early Warning Toolkit (to identify when someone is disconnected and at risk of leaving the team)

- Connection Conversations (to "re-recruit" someone who is feeling disconnected)

- Best and Best and the Aron Closeness Questionnaire (to increase vulnerability and connection)

Make sure to mark this page of the book. Stumped with a connection or relationship problem on your team? Return here, and I think you'll find something useful that will help strengthen relationships on your team and build up your culture.

SETTLING IN, DEALING WITH SETBACKS, AND BRINGING OTHERS ALONG

"You must be the change you want to see in the world."
—Mahatma Gandhi

Once we started the work of transforming the culture with my team, the biggest challenge we faced was accountability. We weren't an accountable culture at all. We rarely accomplished goals (in fact, we rarely set them), we allowed deadlines to slip, and we overlooked or excused weak performance. The crazy thing was we were still getting a lot done. From the outside looking in, you would say we were doing pretty well. But we were a shell of what we could be. We were a shell of what we *would* be just a couple of years later.

Whenever I first introduce the Hero Assumption, I notice the eye rolls. "You should see my team. Not everybody is a hero. And I'm not gonna 'wishful think' my team into some well-oiled machine. I'm not buying it."

Even worse, many times the leader who is convinced to adopt the four shifts rolls out of our workshop and into their department only to hit a brick wall. "Hey, while you were in your fancy-pants training, we were all out here getting our butts kicked. Don't think we don't see through all that psychobabble mumbo jumbo they're teaching you guys."

There is no shortcut to accountability. And it starts with you.

A GAME PLAN FOR INTRODUCING THE FOUR SHIFTS TO YOUR TEAM

If you're going to be successful adopting the four shifts and the behaviors that follow, you'll need a plan. Here are the key elements for a successful implementation of the four shifts in your own team:

1. **Relationships First:** Everything starts with you being personally accountable for your relationships. You cannot hold others accountable until they trust that you see them as the hero of the story and have their best interests at heart.

2. **Personal Accountability:** Next, ask your team to hold you accountable. You earn the privilege of giving feedback and holding others accountable by first showing them that you are open to feedback and being held accountable yourself.

3. **Team Accountability:** Once your team is comfortable that they can trust you and that you want to be accountable to them, you can work on their individual accountabilities. The good news is that if you've laid the above foundation, this begins to take care of itself. You'll probably have to give the process some structure, but the team will be stepping up on their own, learning from your example.

I. RELATIONSHIPS FIRST

Your department is probably a lot like my team was when we started our transformation. You'll have some people with whom you've worked a long time and share a lot of history. They may think they know you well, and you may think you know them well too. Others on your team might be new and have very little history with you or the rest of the team.

If you're like I was, you may want to avoid the difficult relationship stuff and move on to the accountability stuff. But it doesn't work that way. You have to build trust first. Only then can you effectively build accountability.[1]

The last chapter focuses on how to build these relationships, but it is worth repeating that it starts with your willingness to be vulnerable to your team. It's OK to start small with one or two key people. I started with Debbie. Ours was the key relationship that needed to improve, and it wasn't an overnight process. Relationships take time. Over time she needed to see that I was willing to admit to my own shortcomings and that she could safely talk to me about hers (although to be fair, I had more than she did!)

As we built trust with each other, we were able to expand that to others on the team. Remember, we were a small team (probably smaller than your own team), but we weren't that close. Debbie had closer relationships with some members of our team, and I had closer relationships with others. Most of us were blind to what everyone else was doing. So Debbie and I started with the platform of our relationship and expanded that out to the rest of the team.

Over time we built stronger and stronger relationships across the team, using things like Best and Best and the Aron Closeness Questionnaire I discussed in the previous chapter.

YOUR TURN: GRAB BREAKFAST OR LUNCH

In between my law practice and my consulting career, I served as the top human resources officer for a riverboat casino on the Mississippi River in Missouri. As you can probably imagine, there is no shortage of human resources issues on a riverboat casino. And like a lot of organizations, it could be hard for leaders to always have a handle on what was happening on the front line.

One of the things we implemented to help build connections between the front line and top managers was our "Breakfast with the GM" each month. We invited anyone who had a birthday that month to a breakfast where the GM and I would get to know them a little better. We would eat and chat about what was happening in one another's lives. No topic was off-limits. We learned things every month, and it gave us a chance to answer questions and share perspectives in a casual conversation.

The best leaders are approachable. In *The Approachability*

Playbook, I describe the connection model. Leaders connect by being open and available (creating the right space), understanding (creating the right feeling), and supportive (taking the right action). If you're not pouring into each one of those buckets for every member of your team, you lose connection. And that lack of connection can have disastrous consequences on your team and on you as their leader.

But it can be hard to do this consistently. This is even more true now than it was when I wrote *The Approachability Playbook*. So much of our communications have become virtual, and leaders are often stretched to the breaking point.

Now more than ever, it's important to have personal conversations with your team. If you have to get out of the office to do it, then get out of the office. One way I do this is to take every member of my team out for a one-on-one lunch each year around their work anniversary. It's mostly just a chance to eat (I let them pick the spot) and catch up, but I always make a little time for them to talk to me about how things are going, what they'd like to do more of, and what we could do better. I really enjoy this time with each teammate, and it builds trust and makes us closer. And I get to eat at some places I probably never would have tried!

Consider doing something like the "Breakfast with the GM" we did at the casino. Come up with a monthly rotation schedule when you take employees to breakfast or lunch. It's amazing the barriers you can break down simply by getting outside of the office (just like the manager at Google we met in "The 4th Shift").

2. PERSONAL ACCOUNTABILITY

Once Debbie saw that I wanted our relationship to improve and that I was willing to acknowledge my own faults, she got more comfortable giving me feedback. One of the things that rubbed me the wrong way about Debbie was how blunt she was at times. If something was bothering her, it wasn't uncommon for her to blurt it out without really thinking about how it might be received.

When I was making the Villain Assumption about Debbie, I would receive these comments as pointed criticism and out of line. *Who is she to talk to me that way?* I'd think to myself. *She doesn't really understand what I'm working on, so why does she feel like she can comment on it?* Sometimes she'd make these comments in front of others on the team, and I would feel like she was undermining me. That obviously didn't give me warm feelings about her.

As I got to know Debbie better (and she got to know me better), I understood both why she made these comments and why I took them the wrong way. Most of the time, they were a reaction to the fact that I wasn't telling her (or anyone else) what I was working on. I also had a bad habit of recruiting people to help on a project I was working on without asking or even considering whether I was pulling them off some other priority. Since I ran the company, most people didn't feel safe telling me no. This behavior really frustrated Debbie (and others on the team), and I was oblivious.

Once Debbie and I had repaired our relationship, she knew that it was safe to give me blunt feedback. She saw not only that I accepted it, but that I took it to heart and tried to learn and grow from it. From there, she got comfortable holding me accountable for my commitments.

3. TEAM ACCOUNTABILITY

Once you've established that you are willing to receive feedback and be held accountable for your own commitments, you will have invested enough in your relationships to earn the privilege of holding others accountable for their commitments. Again, this is based on building a relationship and a track record of being personally accountable first.

I still have the bad habit of sending people down rabbit trails of my own creation. Recently we did a remodel of our office space. One day on my way home from a client, I was waiting for my flight to take off and ran across the coolest doorstop; I knew it would look great in our updated space (see, that's the kind of shiny object that's likely to grab my attention). I was about to lose connection to the internet, so I quickly sent a Slack* message to Becky in our office, who was helping lead the remodel project. When I landed, I got a Slack from Debbie, which is copied on the following page.

I have committed to the team to "stay in my box" and try to avoid sending them on these wild goose chases. But I still make mistakes. And as you can see, Debbie has no problem holding me accountable for my commitment.

I later showed this Slack exchange to our entire team during my quarterly State of the Company presentation. I did it for several reasons. First, it's a great (if somewhat amusing) example of me not staying in my box and not living up to my accountability. This is something we've asked the team to help me with, and it showed that it was still something we all need to work on—I need to stop diverting people from what they're working on, and the team needs to get better at telling me no.

Debbie 1:54 PM
This kind of stuff makes me crazy. It would have taken you less time to order these yourself.
The slack I receiced from Becky and then she came to my office because we All stop and do whatever Phil wants when he wants it.

Becky [1:44 PM]
Phil wants to order 3 of these for the new upstairs: http://www.amazon.com/2-Pack-Stoppy-Purple-Window-Stopper/dp/B07C82F6R9. Since I don't have A CARD or an Amazon account, can you order these?

Becky doesn't have a company card so she brought Christina into it. Christina doesn't have your amazon login so she couldn't order. So, now I'm involved. A lot of time for something you could have done in less than 30 seconds.
And yes, I'm pounding away on the keyboard which means I should wait a few minutes before sending this and revisit. But how will you know if you're not told?

They have been ordered. You are missed when you're not here and I'm not pounding as hard now ,-)

Phil
Sorry about that. I was losing my internet on the plane. I'll handle now that I have internet. Thank you for the course correction 😊

Debbie 3:34 PM
Don't handle, read what sent. It's been ordered.

And you are missed.

As Debbie mentions in the Slack message, it's not like everyone was sitting around waiting for some request from me. Everyone is working hard, and this was a perfect example of how I can easily derail several people from their true priorities without even thinking about it. Debbie had to coach both Becky and Christina to make sure they pushed back whenever I asked them to divert their attention to something like this. She was able to hold them accountable because she had also earned their trust.

The other reason I showed this whole exchange was because it illustrates that I am comfortable receiving blunt feedback from Debbie. It shows that I want to be held personally accountable for my commitments. I also thought it was good for the whole team to see that Debbie and I are equals and it's safe for her to put me back in my box when I'm out of it.

COACHING PERFORMANCE

As you go through the process of implementing the four shifts in your company, you'll face a number of predictable situations:

1. **Encouraging:** Most of the time you'll be calling attention to the time someone on your team is doing things well (and encouraging them to grow using the Hero Assumption).

2. **Coaching:** Other times someone on your team might be stumbling a bit, and here your role is to coach them and give them feedback to get them on track without discouraging them.

3. **Accountability Discussions:** Occasionally someone on your team will really struggle; they may even be the wrong person in the wrong seat. You'll need tools to navigate these challenging discussions.

ENCOURAGING: HOW TO GIVE (AND HOW NOT TO GIVE) POSITIVE FEEDBACK

Positive feedback can be hard to get right. Some leaders have a hard time giving compliments for day-to-day performance ("Does everybody need a trophy for just doing their job?"). Some don't want to give false praise and worry that if they compliment the same people all the time, it will look like they are playing favorites.

Others are just not very good at giving positive feedback. Their feedback is vague and sounds inauthentic. "Great job today" might feel good the first time you hear it, but if it's the only feedback you get, you begin to wonder if your boss is paying attention to you at all (or if they even know your name!).

Here is a framework for providing positive feedback that is effective and authentic, no matter who you are coaching. You start by looking for some behavior you'd like to see repeated. This might be different for each member of your team.

For newer team members or lower performers, you may want to give encouragement when you catch them doing something right, or when you see them making an effort (even if they're not performing at a high level). More tenured team members might get encouragement for mentoring others, suggesting improvements, or really going above and beyond on certain days. And everyone deserves encouragement when you see them exhibit a core value.

The framework is simple. When you see an employee doing something you want them to repeat in the future or something you want to highlight for others, you should publicly reinforce that behavior. To do so, your feedback must be:

- **Timely**—*When you see it, say it.* Make your observation as close to when you notice the behavior or action as possible.

- **Specific**—*Be concrete, not vague.* Name exactly the action or behavior you want to reinforce or see repeated.

- **Behavior-Focused**—*Always focus on behavior.* Outcomes and motivations aren't in our control or clear enough for effective feedback. Instead, highlight the observable action taken.

- **Repeatable**—If the idea is to get more of it, it must be something that the employee has control over, not just a lucky happenstance.

Whenever you give positive feedback, remember these four key elements.

YOUR TURN: POSITIVE FEEDBACK SCRIPT

Start by listing some behaviors that benefit the organization and the team. You can list key tasks and job duties, but also list things such as core value behaviors (versus the core value itself). Next to each one you list, insert an example of when someone exhibited that behavior.

How do you come up with behaviors that exhibit your core values? At our company, our core values each have a list of four example behaviors that illustrate that core value in action.[2] For example, under our core value of Pursue Excellence, we list: do your best even when you don't have to; challenge yourself and each other; innovate, improve, and sweat the details; and know your stuff and teach others. Those behaviors are things you can observe someone doing.

Your list might look something like this:

Positive Behavior	Recent Example
Sweat the details	Marissa did extra research for a client project
Participate in organizational citizenship behaviors	Joe picked up trash in the parking lot on his way into the office
Innovate	Alex brainstormed a new process to cut down on time for a repeatable task

Once you've got a list of behaviors and recent examples, practice giving positive feedback. This is a great conversation to role-play with a peer who is also in a leadership role. Frame up an "I message" that recognizes a positive behavior, such as one from the prior list. An "I message" is a comment that focuses on what you observed and how it impacted you. Use a script like this:

- "I saw what you did." (Describe the behavior and make it specific.)

- "I appreciate it." (Express gratitude.)

- "It's important." (Explain why the behavior is important to the organization, the team, or to you personally.)

- "It makes me feel . . ." (How did you feel when you saw it?)

Some people aren't so sure about that last "it makes me feel" part. However, your feelings are the most important portion of this script. Remember what you learned in the last chapter about the three questions your employees want to know but never ask? (Do you like me? Do you think I have what it takes? Am I worth the effort?) Using this framework provides an answer to all three questions.

Getting specific and expressing your appreciation conveys warmth and shows that you're paying attention: "You like me!" Explaining why what they did is important to the organization highlights their value and worth: "You think I have what it takes!" Finally, explaining how their behavior moves you emotionally lets them know they are important to you: "I'm worth the effort!" It ensures an emotional connection. It also makes it much more likely they will remember to engage in that behavior in the future.

Using our earlier example, here's what an "I message" might look like:

> Hey Marissa! I just finished that client report [when you see it, say it]. That was a lot of research! Especially that part where you looked back over the prior ten years of financials to spot any trends [be specific; name the behavior]. I really appreciate that extra effort. It shows the client how deep we'll dive to make sure our conclusions are solid, and it makes the whole team look great. I feel proud to hand work like this to the client, and to see how much you've grown. I know I can count on you to make us shine!

Now it's your turn. Grab a partner and practice your own positive feedback. And once you get the hang of it, start handing out positive feedback whenever you can.

COACHING: FEEDBACK ON PERFORMANCE ISSUES USING THE SKILL, AWARENESS, AND VALUES MODEL

One of your team members is failing to live up to their potential. They are making mistakes that are causing delays and quality concerns, making the team look bad and disappointing the customer. What should you do?

Start by making the Hero Assumption. You assume your teammate wants to be great (a vote for Theory Y). Why are they struggling? What's the obstacle getting in the way? What's holding them back on their hero's journey?

A great mental model for this is looking at skill, awareness, and values. This mental model means that if someone isn't living up to their potential, it's a signal that there is a disconnect in one (or more) of three areas:

- **Skill:** They are aware of what's expected, but they don't know how to do it. This is the most common situation, and solving it comes down to just making sure everyone knows how to do what their role requires.

- **Awareness:** They aren't aware of what we expect in a particular situation. For example, we expect the phone to be answered by the second ring, but nobody has explained it to them, and they usually pick up on the third ring.

- **Values:** Their top values aren't consistent with the organization's top values. For example, we value speedy service even if it's not always perfect, but they value doing things deliberately and getting it all exactly right even if it takes a while.

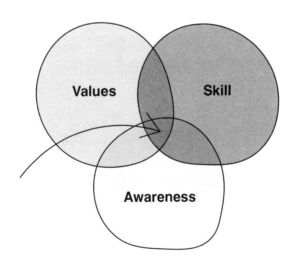

This mental model lets you break down any performance issue in a structured way: Is this a gap in skill, awareness, or values? It helps guide a discussion in a nonjudgmental way if you're not exactly sure what's causing the issue. It also immediately shifts your mindset to Theory Y. There's no judgment here. The leader is simply looking for the gap area and then works with the teammate to help fill it.

Any conversation you have using this model naturally starts with the Hero Assumption: this situation just shows a gap in skill or understanding. Let's examine what happens if any of these three elements is missing.

Using the simple example mentioned earlier, your teammate may value speedy customer service and know how to answer the phone but may not be aware that answering by the second ring is one of the ways the company lives out the speedy customer service value. A lot of times, awareness gaps require just one conversation—once the awareness is there, everything falls into place.

Now, say the teammate is aware of the two-ring rule but struggles with using the phone system, or maybe there isn't a clear handoff when the person who usually picks up is away from their desk. The first one is a skill issue—are there any shortcuts to using the phone system? The second is an awareness issue. A quick conversation can pin it down and easily fill that gap.

What if this person doesn't innately value speedy customer service? These conversations can be more challenging, but resolving a values disconnect is critical. Sometimes a values conversation is a little more like an awareness one; your teammate just doesn't understand how important speedy service is to the organization, because it's not something that bothers them much in their own life.

Other times your teammate may be aware of the value; they just don't share it. This becomes more of a "right person, right seat" conversation. If a value is important to the organization and isn't shared by someone, this will create friction over time.

In our earlier example, someone who really values perfection over speed will struggle in a role that values speed over perfection, no matter how much training they have. If this is someone who otherwise fits the culture, you might consider looking for other roles in the organization where this value mismatch isn't a big deal (the right person moved to a different seat).

On the other hand, if this value is core to every role in the organization, then this isn't the right person for the team. The best way to deal with this is to be direct about what's required. Raise the fact that this role (or any other role you can think of) is going to be a challenge. Ideally, help this person transition to a role that's a better fit, even if it's outside of your team or your organization.

When you must exit a person from the organization, using this model helps focus those conversations as positively as possible. You're still making the Hero Assumption. The fact that someone doesn't share or fit the company values isn't a judgment about them—it's more a failure of the hiring process. Make sure to look at how the mismatch occurred in the first place and figure out what you can do to make sure the same mistake isn't repeated. But you can express confidence that they will be successful somewhere else.

CAN'T, DON'T, OR WON'T? HOW TO TELL IF YOU ARE DEALING WITH A SKILL, AWARENESS, OR VALUES GAP

Here's a quick shortcut to identify whether a situation is a gap in skill, awareness, or values. When you talk to someone about a behavior you've noticed could use improvement, listen carefully for these word pairs:

1. *Can't* or *What*

2. *Don't* or *When*

3. *Won't* or *Why*

How do these six words help you diagnose the type of gap you're dealing with?

Can't or *What* (or sometimes *How*) indicates you are dealing with a skill gap. If someone knows when and why to do something (they have awareness and value the behavior), then the only reason they aren't following through is a skill gap. They don't know what or how to do what's being asked. If someone says, "I *can't* do that," or "Nobody showed me *what* to do" (or "Nobody showed me *how* to do that"), you know you are dealing with a skill issue.

Don't or *When* indicates an awareness gap. If someone knows what to do and why it's important, then a lack of follow-through is probably an awareness issue. If someone says, "I *don't* handle it that way," or "I'm not sure *when* that's supposed to happen," they are signaling a lack of awareness.

Won't or *Why* is a sign you're dealing with a values disconnect. If someone knows what to do and when to do it, a lack of follow-through shows that the employee probably isn't sure why that behavior is important. If someone says, "I *won't* ever do it that way," or asks, "*Why* do we do it this way?" they are indicating they don't understand why a behavior is important to the organization.

The next time you're in a coaching conversation, listen for the word pairs: *Can't* or *What*, *Don't* or *When*, or *Won't* or *Why*.

YOUR TURN: PRACTICE SKILL, AWARENESS, AND VALUES CONVERSATIONS

Think back to the last five performance coaching conversations you've had. On the left-hand side of this table, list the issue you had to discuss. Next to that, list whether you think that topic is primarily a gap in skill, awareness, or values:

Performance-Related Conversation	Skill, Awareness, or Values?

For each behavior, practice having a conversation using the Skill, Awareness, and Values diagram. During your conversation, practice writing out the Venn diagram, and ask for help with your teammate to diagnose which of the three areas they think is the problem. Then come up with a plan to shrink the gap and make a plan to follow up.

OTHER CONSTRUCTIVE FEEDBACK TOOLS

In addition to the Skill, Awareness, and Values mental model and Venn diagram, there are a few other tools you can also use to communicate performance expectations.

THE RESULTS/VALUES MATRIX

The Results/Values Matrix helps you communicate with someone who is failing to meet performance expectations. Focus your discussions on task performance (results) or culture fit issues (values). You can use this tool anytime, but it's especially useful when the results or values issues could jeopardize an employee's continued employment.

Start by plotting out where the person fits across the dimensions of results and values on a matrix that looks like this:

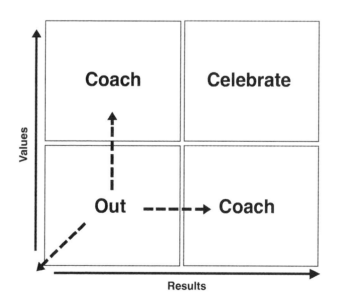

Think of the Results/Values Matrix as an overall performance map. You plot your teammate's performance across two dimensions:

1. **Results:** *How much do they accomplish or produce?* This dimension is focused on productivity, irrespective of HOW they achieve those results.

2. **Values:** *How do they accomplish their results?* This ignores the actual amount produced and focuses instead on how well they fit the core values of the organization and how well they treat their teammates.

When someone is struggling, this is a simple way to focus a coaching conversation on the most important areas for improvement. Each person will fall into one of four quadrants. In the top-right quadrant, you are dealing with a star employee—someone who produces a lot and does it the right way. These are folks you want to celebrate and encourage to keep up the great work. They should be held up as an example to others.

For an employee in the bottom-right box, you are coaching on values. This is someone whose results are good, but the way they get those results needs work. A performance improvement discussion with this individual could focus on things like how they treat teammates or customers, attention to quality, or integrity concerns.

An employee in the top-left box needs coaching on results. They are the "right person" doing things the right way; they're just not doing enough of them! A performance improvement discussion with someone in this box will focus on production and daily task performance. Here you'll want to make sure that results expectations are clear and accountability is in place.

Finally, you may have someone in the bottom-left box, which we call the Out box. This means they are not meeting expectations on their results *or* their values. These are your most serious performance discussions because for someone here, you'll need to begin discussing the consequences of failing to improve.

You'll see the three arrows in the Out box. There are three ways out of the box: improving results, improving values, or exiting the company. All three should be discussed with team members in the Out box. (Later in this chapter, we cover discussions that could lead to discipline or an exit from the company.)

This tool is useful because it is a great visual representation of overall performance. It illustrates that you can't just do well in one of the dimensions. When you sit down with your teammate, you can draw a matrix like this one and plot them across the two dimensions. You can even ask them to plot where they would put themselves on the map and see if there is disagreement.

Once you roughly agree on where they are on the map—and ultimately you get to decide—you then discuss how to plot the course to the top-right box. This is a great visual representation of the hero's journey ahead. And in follow-up conversations, you can show progress by plotting a new point on the matrix. It's a great, practical, visual tool for targeted performance improvement discussions.

YOUR TURN: COACHING SCRIPT: "I'VE NOTICED SOMETIMES . . ."

Many performance issues aren't serious enough to warrant a Results/Values discussion. It's just something you notice that you want to raise awareness about. It might be getting distracted by personal calls at work or being too interested in the latest office gossip.

For situations like these, you want to use the "I've noticed sometimes . . ." script. If you are making the Hero Assumption and notice someone engaging in negative or distracting behavior, your first thought should be that they aren't aware of the impact they are having. These conversations will normally center around awareness and perhaps values.

The idea here is to make it clear you are not judging the individual. Nobody wants to feel judged. Instead, remain in the mindset that you've noticed a behavior and you want to make sure they've noticed it too. To do that, you always start by saying, "I've noticed sometimes . . ."

1. "I've noticed sometimes your questions about someone's personal life can get awkward."

2. "I've noticed sometimes your time talking about fantasy football distracts others from their work."

3. "I've noticed sometimes your frequent smoke breaks make you unavailable when people need you."

4. "I've noticed sometimes your choice of humor can make people feel uncomfortable."

"I've noticed sometimes . . ." says that while you've noticed an issue, it happens sometimes, not all the time. It also presents the issue as one of awareness. You're acknowledging this may be something they're completely unaware of. Even if they are generally aware, they may not be fully aware of how noticeable it is or the impact it's having on the team. Presenting coaching feedback this way creates a low-intensity opportunity to quickly correct issues.

Once you state what you've noticed, pause. Give your teammate a chance to react and respond. Giving them this space is important. Often, they'll immediately acknowledge the issue and suggest some changes going forward. Other times, they might be defensive or try to explain away either the behavior or the impact.

However they handle it, give them some space to explain what the situation looks like from their point of view. If you feel like they're not getting it, you'll need to redirect the conversation using the next coaching script.

YOUR TURN: COACHING SCRIPT: SOLUTION-FOCUSED QUESTIONS

Let's say you've started to give some feedback using the "I've noticed sometimes" coaching script and your teammate gets defensive (I call it "getting their defense on the field"). This is a signal they are feeling singled out or judged. They may:

1. **Stall** or brush it off to avoid the discussion ("Oh, sure, I'll work on that.")

2. **Divert** the conversation by trying to make you feel sorry for them ("I'm such a dope—why do I keep doing stuff like that?" or even the passive-aggressive "Sorry I'm not doing a good enough job for you.")

3. **Challenge** the feedback ("Oh, it's easy for you to say from your office, but I'm out here having to do all the work.")

These are normal reactions, but they are all ways to avoid having an important conversation. Don't let yourself get sidetracked.

At times like these, it's important to remember what you learned about acceptance: "I like you." "You have what it takes." "You're worth the effort." Right now you're not talking about something disciplinary. Instead, you just want to make sure to refocus on the issue and then start thinking about a solution.

If your teammate tries to divert the conversation, you can refocus it by reminding your teammate that you like and respect them. "I'm not the kind of person who will let you walk around all day with spinach in your teeth, and I hope you'd do the same for me. I'm only bringing it up because I figured you weren't aware of it." A lot of times awareness is the natural end to the conversation. If it comes up again, you can mention it, but many times, that's it. Problem solved.

Other times the issue is a little more involved. Your teammate might need some support in becoming more self-aware. They may need accountability to notice this in the future. There may also be times when your teammate needs encouragement to build a new skill. They may ask you to role-play with them or help them find some training. This is the time for a pivot to solution-focused questions.

A solution-focused question concentrates on the best response to a problem versus the problem itself. It's hard not to feel judged if your boss is centering the conversation on the problem. But if you turn attention to the solution, the discussion quickly becomes collaborative and productive. Examples of solution-focused questions include:

- What do we hope to accomplish?

- What do we need?

- What could make this better?

- If this was easy, how would we do it?

- Who can help?

- How can I help?

- What's next? What can we do now to move this forward?

By the way, solution-focused questions are useful in a lot of situations. Embedded in here are the Three Questions asked by Approachable Leaders.[3] Anytime you are presented with a problem, look at that as a signal to start asking solution-focused questions. Concentrating on problems often leads to judgment and blame: "Why are we facing this problem? Who caused it? What is it costing us?" It creates defensiveness and negativity. The energy in a room transforms when you pivot from problems to solutions.

ACCOUNTABILITY DISCUSSIONS: YOU CAN'T STAY IN THE OUT BOX

Most performance-related coaching can be handled with the tools mentioned earlier. Often when you give someone feedback, they'll correct the behavior. It might take some time and an occasional course correction, but they are generally moving toward the top-right box on the Values/Results Matrix.

Rarely but occasionally, you'll come across someone who remains stubbornly stuck in the Out box. They just don't seem willing or able to take the steps they need to move up in either values or results. This requires you to have an accountability discussion.

Accountability discussions are more serious. If proper action isn't taken, it will lead to separation of employment.[4] That's because you cannot, for the sake of the team and the organization, allow someone to languish in the Out box. It's not fair to the team, who are all being held to a higher standard. It's not fair to the organization.

It's also not fair to the individual who, for whatever reason, is stuck in a role they can't or won't do well at an organization whose values they don't line up with. It's a miserable way to live. And even though losing a job is tough in the short term, it can be a blessing in disguise by providing a chance to find a role in which they can thrive.

When you are faced with a situation like this, is it time to stop making the Hero Assumption? No! There is no more important time to make the Hero Assumption than when the going gets tough.

Remember, this employee's hero's journey (and your hero's journey, for that matter) is not over. In many cases, a serious disciplinary situation is the obstacle that, once overcome, is the key moment in launching a successful employee's career. And in those cases where the journey is going to continue at another company, you still want to handle the departure in a way that says you continue to believe in them. Who knows, one day their journey may bring them back to you.

When dealing with situations that could lead to discipline or an exit from the company, you should continue to treat them as the hero. However, your focus turns to how they are not living up to expectations. You can restate your belief that they have what it takes. At the same time, they must understand that your belief in them does not mean they aren't accountable. You can believe in them and still be forced to remove them from the team.

YOUR TURN: COACHING SCRIPT: ACCOUNTABILITY DISCUSSION

When you are having an accountability discussion, it is vital to be clear about these four areas:

1. The specific behavior that needs to change
2. The employee's commitment to change the behavior
3. How and when to evaluate progress
4. The consequences if progress isn't made

Before you have an accountability discussion, be clear on points one and four. State the behavior that needs to change as plainly as you can. Make sure the behavior is observable and something the employee can control. Also be clear about what will happen if that behavior doesn't change.

Points two and three will normally get fleshed out during the discussion. But you might also consider what types of commitments you think would fix the situation, and how and when you will measure whether progress is being made. Some situations allow you to see progress quickly, while others might need to be evaluated over weeks or months.

After you've thought about the four points, it is time to hold the discussion. Accountability discussions should be held in private. Do it at a time and place where you can avoid distractions and interruptions. Here is a script to follow:

- **Observe:** "This is what I've observed . . ."

- **Respond:** Pause and let them respond. Listen for defensiveness (see the previous script for solution-focused questions for tips).

- **Commit:** "What do you commit to do?" Let them define their commitment.

  » If you don't believe their initial commitment will fix the situation, work together to create an effective and attainable commitment using solution-focused questions.

- **Restate:** Once you've agreed on a commitment that will work, restate the commitment. "What you're committing to do is. . . . Do I have that right?"

- **Follow Up:** "How will we know and when should we check in to make sure this is solved?" Let them define how and when you'll measure progress.

  » If you don't believe their initial "how and when" proposal will fix the situation, work together on a commitment using solution-focused questions.

  » Once you've agreed on a "how and when" commitment that will work, restate the commitment. "What you're committing to do is. . . . Do I have that right?"

- **Ask How You Can Help:** "This is your commitment, and I believe you will make it happen. Let me know how I can help."

  » Offer any help you think is appropriate but listen for signals that they aren't accepting this as their responsibility.

  » If you feel they aren't accepting accountability, reiterate to them that they are solely responsible for following through. You will help however you can, but it is their job to follow through.

Defensiveness during an accountability discussion is a problem. It creates wiggle room and reduces clarity. If you experience defensiveness (the stall, the brush-off, the diversion, or the challenge), you'll need to make sure it's clear that none of these excuses change the commitment.

In this case, you deal with defensiveness by simply going back to the starting point: name the behavior. After any excuse (even if there are several—and during an accountability discussion, there often are), simply state: "I understand; nevertheless, this is what I've observed." You can change the words slightly; however, "I understand, nevertheless . . ." is tried-and-true.

Once you've reached a commitment using the provided script, it's important to follow up. Even if you've seen that the behavior has improved, make sure you follow through with the conversation you committed to in step four. Even if it's just a chance to celebrate how well things are going, it's important for the employee to know that the commitment was real, that you've noticed how they were doing, and that it remains important.

Confidently handling discussions like these is a sign of a true leader. They can be stressful, but they are important. You can turn around a teammate who is train-wrecking the culture (and possibly keep other valuable team members from leaving). In some cases, you'll turn around someone's career. It can even transform your own career—the leader of a floundering or imploding team is not making the short list of high-potential promotions.

These conversations don't always succeed. Sometimes the problem isn't fixable. An employee who doesn't share the core values of the organization or can't (or won't) perform as expected is ultimately not a fit and eventually needs to go. Often they'll quit, knowing it's never going to work. Sometimes they'll be fired.

However, in most cases I've been involved in, an employee who has received accountability discussions isn't surprised and is sometimes even relieved. It's never easy, but everyone knows by that point that we've really tried to make it work. They understand that they are the ones at fault. And we can then focus on the "What's next?" part of the journey.

SUMMING UP: HOW DO I KNOW IF I'M DOING THIS RIGHT?

Remember the Dunning-Kruger diagram? If my journey over the last few years has taught me anything, it's that I *always* assume I'm at the top of Mount Stupid. That way I never think I have all the answers, and I'm always looking to learn and grow more as a leader. This leadership stuff is hard—I'd put it right up there with parenting as the hardest but most high-impact thing you'll ever do.

My wife, Janet, is a swim coach, mostly working with people training for a triathlon. When she teaches people how to swim in open water, one of the first things she has to teach is "sighting." It's really easy to get disoriented when you're in open water, which, if you're not a great swimmer, can be very dangerous. So she teaches new open-water swimmers to always pick a target to swim toward, like a buoy or a landmark on the opposite shoreline. Then she coaches them to regularly sight: to pull their heads up at the end of a stroke to reorient and make sure they are swimming toward their target.

This is how I think about my own leadership journey. During my normal day-to-day, I am head down in the water, swimming hard and dealing with whatever waves or obstacles come my way. I am heading generally in the direction I've started, but depending on the conditions, I could easily end up off course. That's when it's important for me to sight—to take a pause, reorient, and ask:

- How is my team doing?
- Is there anyone I haven't checked in with in a while?
- Who's killing it?
- Who's challenged?
- How am I doing? Is there anything I should be working on?

When you're swimming in open water, it can be lonely. Even if you're swimming with other people, they can't really help you swim the course. You have to do that on your own. Leadership can be a lot like that. It can feel lonely.

The good news is that leadership doesn't have to be lonely. Unlike a swimmer in open water, you can ask for help and get feedback from your mentors, those who have traveled the trail ahead of you. You can even get feedback from your peers or your teammates who are traveling the trail with you.

In this chapter, I offer you a lot of practical tools you can put into practice in your everyday leadership. However, as you learned in the introduction, leadership isn't really about the tools. It's about your mindset. If you get your mindset right, it will guide your behavior and your actions. That's why you need to occasionally sight. Check in with yourself and make sure you are in the Hero Assumption mindset.

If you notice you are making the Villain Assumption about someone on your team (or in your life), that's a signal you need to reorient. Seek out that person and check in. Be vulnerable. Let them know you care about the relationship and share how you are feeling. These are some of the most important conversations you can have.

It wasn't that long ago that I thought I was a pretty solid leader, skilled enough that I could write a book about it and teach thousands of people how to do it. I do feel like I've come a long way as a leader over the last few years. But where am I now? Just to be safe, I'm assuming I'm on the peak of another Mount Stupid.

I don't have all the answers. Nobody does. But the answers are out there. They are in the relationships you grow with your team. "Am I doing this right?" That's the wrong question. Do your best each day and make the Hero Assumption about yourself and your team. Sight and reorient by focusing on your relationships and your mindset. You'll end up right on target.

HOW THE HERO ASSUMPTION IMPROVES YOUR LIFE

"Knowledge is the beginning of practice;
doing is the completion of knowing."
—**Wang Yangming, ancient Chinese philosopher**

"I got my bags packed, son. I got my bags packed."

Jim Valvano had a dream: one day he would coach a team to win a national championship. And 1983 was his best chance yet. Valvano's dream started in high school. His dad, Rocco, was his basketball coach, and Jim dreamed of following in his father's footsteps. One day Jim got an assignment to write some goals on a notecard. One of his goals was to coach a team to an NCAA championship. When Jim told his dad about his dream, Rocco said, "Well, I got my bags packed, son. I got my bags packed."

Valvano got his first NCAA coaching job in 1972. In celebration and anticipation, Valvano's dad took him up to his bedroom and showed him a suitcase. "See that suitcase? I got my bags packed." Rocco would repeat this phrase to Jim many more times over his coaching career.

Prior to joining the Wolfpack, Valvano coached five seasons at Iona College where his team qualified for the NCAA basketball tournament in 1979 and 1980. When Valvano went home to celebrate with his family, his dad showed him the suitcase again. "I got my bags packed, son. I got my bags packed."

Valvano's Iona teams never advanced past the second round, and he was picked to coach North Carolina State for the following season. There was no more reason to believe Valvano would coach North Carolina State to a national championship than there was when he was at Iona. Nevertheless, his father kept on believing. And in 1982, when the Wolfpack qualified for their first NCAA tournament under Valvano, his dad said, "I got my bags packed, son. I got my bags packed."

The Wolfpack lost in the first round.

Valvano's 1983 Wolfpack team had three seniors, and the season began with high hopes. But in the very first game, their star senior forward broke his foot. The wheels fell off. By the time the regular season ended, the Wolfpack had lost ten games, and there was virtually no chance they would make it into the national tournament, much less win the championship.

Miraculously, North Carolina State did qualify for the NCAA tournament by winning the ACC championship. They had to beat the number five- and two-ranked teams in the nation. The Wolfpack cut the nets and were going to the NCAA tournament.

Valvano and his scrappy Wolfpack team were huge underdogs. They were a six seed, which had never won a championship game before then. But Rocco Valvano didn't care about a meaningless stat like that. At a family dinner just before the tournament, Rocco called Jim upstairs and showed him the suitcase. "I got my bags packed, son. We're going to the national championship."

The Wolfpack nearly lost in the first round, going into overtime. They kept winning nail-biting last-minute upsets that earned the team the nickname "Cardiac Pack." After once again beating a dominant Virginia team, Valvano's Cinderella team advanced to the Final Four.

The Wolfpack advanced to the final, facing their most daunting challenge of the year. Their opponent Houston was one of the most talented college basketball teams in history, boasting a lineup with two future NBA Hall of Famers. Valvano's team consisted of prohibitive underdogs. If they could win, it would be one of the largest point-spread upsets in tournament history.

Once again, the Wolfpack would need a miracle to make their championship dream come true. After Valvano's team took a surprising eight-point lead into halftime, the Cougars roared back in the second half, leading by seven. But the Cardiac Pack scratched back to a tie late in the game. Down by one point with five seconds left, their star forward launched an improbable shot at the basket from half-court. It missed. But as time expired, their center tipped the ball in. The Wolfpack won the national championship.

Valvano believed his team would succeed in the tournament. He believed they could win a national championship the same way his dad believed Valvano could win a national championship. "My bags are packed," he always said.

Even during the darkest parts of that 1983 season, when his team wasn't living up to their potential, Valvano never wavered in his belief. He said that after they won the ACC tournament, he could tell that the team was finally beginning to believe in themselves. They started seeing what their coach had seen all along. When asked, "Are you a team of destiny?" they answered, "Yes." They felt like they were destined to win the tournament. This is the Hero Assumption at its greatest. It's creating a belief that ultimately fulfills a prophecy.

What strikes me most about that story isn't the incredible Cinderella victory. It's Valvano's belief and positive attitude and his ability to overcome all the doubt and darkness. He came by that naturally. After all, Rocco had been making the Hero Assumption about Jim his whole life.

HOW THE HERO ASSUMPTION AFFECTS YOUR WORK LIFE (AND YOUR RESULTS)

This book tells the story of four shifts I made in my leadership journey, and by far the most important shift was to make the Hero Assumption. The Hero Assumption isn't just for leadership at work. Valvano's Wolfpack team won an improbable NCAA championship with a heavy dose of the Hero Assumption. But the research makes clear your day-to-day work life is much better when you make the Hero Assumption. Running around each day, hounding all those "villains" on your team in your Theory X T-shirt is a recipe for bad days at work for everyone. It increases stress for you and your team. It tanks everyone's productivity. And it's guaranteed to run off your best talent.

The Hero Assumption is a critical component of being an

approachable leader. It's the "foundation to the foundation." When you make the Hero Assumption, you'll automatically behave like an approachable leader.

When I finished *The Approachability Playbook* in 2016, I included a brief chapter at the end called "The Case for Leader Approachability." That chapter, based on research done by Cameron G. Brown when he wrote his dissertation, outlined the primary benefits of leader approachability.

Cameron's dissertation identified several key findings.[1] Employees of approachable leaders reported high job satisfaction (and employees with unapproachable leaders reported low job satisfaction) 88.5 percent of the time. They were 73.5 percent more likely to go above and beyond at work. They felt they had a voice in the workplace (a key motivator of young workers) 75 percent of the time. And they were 74 percent less likely to want to leave their job, a dramatic reduction in turnover intention.

In May 2021 Dr. Josh Royes and I updated this research.[2] This study used a large survey sample (more than 7,200 participants) to further substantiate that approachability is an important predictor of turnover intention, organizational citizenship behavior (OCB), and organization satisfaction. This link is important because turnover can be extremely costly to an organization. In this study, approachable leadership was associated with increased OCB, even when controlling for workplace conditions satisfaction and pay satisfaction.

This most recent study showed similar size effects. In the following chart, you see the correlation between leader approachability (or unapproachability) and satisfaction, turnover, and organizational citizenship.

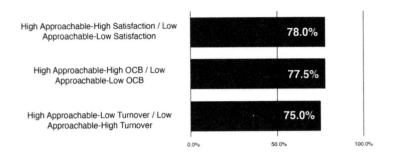

Approachablity Size Effects on Satisfaction, OCB, and Turnover

Leader approachability is highly correlated with reduced turnover, higher organizational citizenship, and improved overall satisfaction.

The three main drivers of approachability (receptivity, availability, and warmth) in both studies are directly improved by the Hero Assumption. It's why we teach this concept in all three of our Approachable Leadership Workshops, and why our second workshop is dedicated entirely to the Hero Assumption.

One of the more powerful findings in Dr. Brown's research was that the benefits of these leadership traits are not situational. He concluded, "Instead, approachability largely appeared to be equally beneficial across individuals and situations."[3] This is why learning these behaviors is so important. No matter the situation (new employee, seasoned employee, highly skilled, or just getting started), these tools will help.

MAKE MORE MONEY: A BETTER WORK LIFE AND A FATTER BANK ACCOUNT?

MetLife had a serious problem. They were burning through sales reps.[4]

In the early 1980s, MetLife received more than sixty thousand applications for new life insurance salespeople. After testing, screening, and interviewing, they offered jobs to five thousand of these applicants. They then spent more than thirty thousand dollars training each agent, but after one year, half the agents were gone. After four years, only about one thousand were left. MetLife was bleeding more than a million dollars a year in hiring costs.

Insurance sales is extremely difficult and churns through talent at an extraordinary rate. Each salesperson deals with rejection constantly. And MetLife was desperately hoping to solve the riddle of how to find people who were the most likely to succeed. They didn't just want to avoid the expense of training so many people just to see them fail—they hoped to avoid the human cost of burning through all this talent every year.

They decided to take a chance on a professor who'd been studying a new subject area called positive psychology. Martin Seligman from the University of Pennsylvania studied how "learned optimism" (the opposite of "learned helplessness") might be the answer to MetLife's problems. Learned optimism is basically making the Hero Assumption—looking at the glass as half-full and using that to overcome challenges.

Seligman had developed a process to identify optimists and pessimists. His research had already proven that pessimists are likely to easily give up when faced with a challenge and are also more likely to become depressed when handling rejection. You'd be hard-pressed to find a more challenging or rejection-filled career than life insurance sales. Seligman hypothesized that highly optimistic people should be the most likely to succeed at a career like this.

MetLife decided to use Seligman's questionnaire to analyze current salespeople. Their first test suggested that looking for optimists might be the right approach: agents who scored in the optimistic half of the questionnaire sold 37 percent more than the bottom half, and the top 10 percent of optimists sold 88 percent more than the bottom 10 percent.

Further, they found that agents who scored in the bottom half of the questionnaire were twice as likely to quit than those in the top half. Also, agents in the bottom quartile quit three times more than those in the top. Optimism scores were more predictive than either career profile or intelligence scores.

In 1985 MetLife decided to let Seligman's team look at the performance of new hires. That year, potential agents took the standard career profile test and the optimism questionnaire. Seligman's team then studied a cohort of one thousand agents who passed the career profile. Half the agents in this cohort were optimists and half were pessimists. The team also looked at an additional cohort of one hundred "special agents." These special agents *failed* the normal career profile (and would normally never be hired) but scored in the top half of the optimism scale.

Over the next two years, Seligman's team studied the results of these two cohorts. In year one, the first cohort, the optimists, barely outperformed the pessimists (8 percent better). In year two, the optimists improved, selling 31 percent more than the pessimists.

The results among the "special agents" were even more pronounced. These agents (who, remember, would never have been hired under the normal career profile) outperformed the regular agents by 21 percent in year one and 57 percent in year two. Optimism predicted sales performance more than any other factor.

Making the Hero Assumption about yourself pays big financial dividends in your life, and this effect compounds over time. I'm not saying it will make you rich. But it clearly helps along the way. And making the Villain Assumption puts unnecessary obstacles in the way of your financial achievement.

MAKE THE HERO ASSUMPTION, MAKE MORE MONEY

I often start my leadership keynotes by asking, "OK, show of hands—how many of you would like to make more money?" Would you raise your hand? Then I've got great news. The glass half-full people who make the Hero Assumption are also financially more successful than the glass half-empty folks.

We've already seen that optimists make better salespeople. But they are also just generally more financially successful. Positive psychologist Michelle Gielan makes the case in a 2019 *Harvard Business Review* article.[5] Among the findings:

- Optimists experience better financial health than pessimists—they save more, are more likely to have an emergency fund, and are much less stressed about money.

- Optimists spend less time looking for a job and are much more likely to be hired than pessimists.

- Optimists are both choosier and more likely to be promoted.[6]

People who exhibit dispositional optimism (in other words, choosing or naturally adopting an optimistic mindset such as making the Hero Assumption) are financially more successful. If you are the kind of leader who cares about job satisfaction, employee voice, above-and-beyond behavior at work, lower turnover, and a fat bank account, the answer is clear: work on making the Hero Assumption part of your everyday leadership tool kit.

HOW THE HERO ASSUMPTION IMPROVES YOUR LOVE LIFE

These impacts don't stop as you leave work each day. The exact same behaviors influence whether you are likely to be successful in a romantic relationship. Just like in the Pygmalion myth itself—if you look at your significant other through rose-colored glasses (also known as "positive illusions"), your relationship is likely to thrive. Zenger and Folkman explain:

> This was a meta-analysis of 137 studies collected over 33 years with 37,761 participants [that looked] at factors that cause non-married couples to break up or stay together. The number one factor that kept people together was something they called "positive illusion"—essentially that the person you're dating thinks you're awesome.[7]

How would you like to experience a satisfying, long-term relationship with few conflicts? Do you want to feel confident about your relationship and secure about yourself and your partner? Avoid a breakup? A 2019 paper summarizing research on relationships found that:

[I]ndividuals with higher positive illusions of their relationship enjoy higher relationship satisfaction, less conflicts and doubts, and decreased risk for relationship discontinuation.[8]

If you make the Hero Assumption about your spouse, you are much more likely to remain together. And if you are a hard grader? That's not going to end well.

It's easy to blame the other person when we get into an argument (what one study calls the "reign of error"), but the research suggests it is often our own mindset that triggers a conflict or a fight. Another meta-study concludes that "anticipated acceptance"—assuming others will accept us warmly—triggers warm interactions.[9] And you guessed it: if you anticipate rejection or a cold interaction, that's exactly what you get.

HOW THE HERO ASSUMPTION IMPROVES YOUR HEALTH AND WELL-BEING

If I offered you a pill that was proven to increase your lifespan by three to eight years, would you want to learn more? What if that pill also made you more likely to live past the age of eighty-five?

Since you already know all about the nocebo effect, I guess I should warn you that this pill does have some side effects. In addition to making you live longer, it also improves your love life, your financial wellness, and your leadership. Sound familiar?

Scientists are carefully studying the benefits of dispositional optimism on health, and the results are astounding. In one study, women who were optimistic saw their lifespans increase by 5 percent.[10] In another study, male optimists lived 11 percent longer than pessimists.[11] That's a three-year increase in lifespan for women and an eight-year increase for men.

Both studies found that optimists are much more likely to achieve "exceptional longevity" (living to the age of eighty-five or older). One found that 53 percent of optimists achieved exceptional longevity, and that's after controlling for other lifestyle factors like smoking, wealth, etc. that can skew results in longevity studies like these.

Dispositional optimism is also associated with better mental health. Studies show that optimists have a lower risk of depressive episodes[12] and a lower likelihood of suicidal ideation.[13]

You've probably heard the saying, "You're only as old as you feel." Well, it's true. Your beliefs about aging have a big impact on how you'll experience old age. In one recent study, older individuals were measured on their beliefs about aging. And then twenty-three years passed. Participants with a positive self-perception of aging lived seven and a half years longer than those who had negative beliefs about aging.[14] This advantage remained even after controlling for age, gender, socioeconomic status, loneliness, and functional health.

In another study, participants primed with negative stereotypes about aging experienced signs of cardiac stress (higher blood pressure, increased heart rate) versus those exposed to positive stereotypes on aging.[15] You could improve your heart health and add nearly ten years to your life by simply making the Hero Assumption about how you'll age.

WHAT'S NEXT? MAKING THE HERO ASSUMPTION IN *YOUR* LIFE

You're convinced (see, I'm a dispositional optimist): the Hero Assumption is vitally important. It's important for your work as a leader. It's important for your personal relationships and your love life. It's important for your financial well-being. And it's important for your health.

You know how to do it. This book has dozens of practical tools, exercises, and references that can help you apply the Hero Assumption in your life.

But before you leave, I have two last questions:

- Who has their bags packed for you?
- For whom do you have your bags packed?

In the last year, I lost two really important people to me. One of them was my high school debate coach, Jeanne Devilliers (or Dee). When I walked into Dee's classroom, I found my place—a place where I belonged, built confidence, and had what it takes. Dee believed in me. That led me down a path of debating in college and then going to law school. I never would have done any of that if I hadn't met Dee. And I let her down.

My junior year I was caught drinking at an overnight debate tournament. I ended up expelled from school and suspended from the team for the biggest tournament of the year. I let Dee and my team down. She was embarrassed, angry, and disappointed. But she never gave up on me. She never lost belief. And that gave me the confidence to later succeed in a way I never imagined. Dee made the Hero Assumption about me.

145

I also lost my friend Austin Clary. You met Austin briefly earlier in the book (he always taught me to "assume positive intent"). Austin was a work colleague, but I knew him as a kid. He worked for my dad, and I always looked up to him. We later worked together for a number of years.

One of the things I always admired about Austin was that he had high standards. He was hard to work with sometimes because he would push everyone around him to not just be their best but to work at a standard that sometimes felt unnecessarily high. He always made everyone around him better, though, including me. He believed so much in people. He believed so much in me. And I didn't fully appreciate that while he was here.

When Austin said to assume positive intent, he was saying to make the Hero Assumption. If somebody frustrates or confuses you, assuming positive intent changes how you react. And that was Austin. At his very best, he really helped leaders and teammates understand that in any situation there's an opportunity to learn and grow.

I never told Dee or Austin that my bags were packed for them. And I never really thanked them for having their bags packed for me. That's my final request to you as you begin your own hero's journey. Think about those for whom you've packed your bags. Let them know wherever they are on their journey that you're right there with them. Let them know your bags are packed.

Also, think about those who have packed their bags for you. Let them know how much you appreciate their confidence in you and that they believed in you even when you may not have believed in yourself. Do it while you still can.

Finally, make sure you have your bags packed for yourself. Leadership is hard and can be lonely. Even when you're doing it well, it's easy to get discouraged. That's when you have to fill yourself up with some dispositional optimism and make the Hero Assumption about yourself.

I know you can do it. I've got my bags packed for you.

—PHIL

ACKNOWLEDGMENTS

There are so many people who helped me get this book to the finish line. Without them this project would never have been possible.

First, I want to thank my team. You've already met some of them, and I could fill several more books with the journey of how our team has grown and developed over the last four years. Everyone in our organization has served as the inspiration for this book and has given me the encouragement and space to write (and rewrite). I'd like to thank our leadership team (Debbie Barnett, whom you met in the book, along with Danine Clay, Eric Funston, and Greg Kittinger) and our "Traction Team" (Becky Frank and Laura Wright, who also appear in the book, and Christina Jochmans, Erin Lormer, Mai Yang, Britani Bird, Lindsey Swisher, and Michael VanDervort). I'd especially like to thank Debbie, who has been so important to my own growth and development as a leader. This journey would not be possible without your partnership.

This is the second book where I've turned to publishing strategist and writer Janet Goldstein for her invaluable guidance. I had a first draft written when I asked her to help. It was a hot mess (she wasn't that blunt, but it's true). Janet challenged me to sharpen the message and pushed me to dig deep into how I had put these lessons to work in my own life. I rewrote it two more times based on her excellent suggestions and (usually) gentle prodding. It may not be perfect, but be glad you're reading this version!

This is the third book I've worked on with Meghan Jones (Debbie Barnett's wonderfully talented daughter). Meghan was again invaluable in drafting and rewriting this book. She's been alongside me during the whole development and launch of our Approachable Leadership body of work, and she challenges me to do my best work (like her mom). It's been an honor to work with Meghan over the years and been so cool to watch her grow into the amazing mother and writer she's become. She knows I've got my bags packed for her.

This is the first book I've done with a publisher and publicist, and I'm so grateful that Janet Goldstein introduced me to the folks at Greenleaf and Smith Publicity. The superb team of professionals at Greenleaf were a pleasure to work with. The book looks and reads so much better under their care and guidance. And the team at Smith Publicity has been a terrific help in helping me get the word out about the book and our work at Approachable Leadership.

I'd also like to thank my "kitchen cabinet" of friends and colleagues I've leaned on for feedback and reaction to many of the ideas I cover in the book. Leny Riebli, Mike Esposito, Daren Wingard, David Haddad, Nick Kalm, Fiona Jamison, Terry Dunn, Mike Perkins, Greg Kittinger, Rick Farr, and Steve Wardrop were all great sounding boards and big fans of the concepts in this book. Nancy Jowske gifted me a copy of *The Hero with a Thousand Faces* many years ago, and we've had spirited discussions about leadership over the years, which have sharpened my thinking, especially the importance of empathy and humility. I got to watch Cameron Brown and Josh Royes each earn their PhDs while helping me add rigor and hard research to what many consider a "soft" subject. I appreciate the inspiration, support, and counsel each of you has given me over the years.

You met Nate Brim at the beginning of this book, and I want to thank him for his guidance, encouragement, and counsel throughout the journey I describe in the book. He's been such a great resource to our team and a great friend to me. My life is so much better with you in it.

I want to thank my mom and dad. Just like Jim Valvano's parents, you both have had your bags packed for me my whole life. Mom, you've always made the Hero Assumption about me and encouraged me to be my best. And Dad, you've inspired me, and you laid the foundation for everything I've been able to accomplish. Our company wouldn't exist without you, and I've learned so much from you over the years. I hope I've made both of you proud.

Finally, I want to thank Janet and Marissa, my wife and daughter. You've borne the brunt of me testing ideas and sharing (way too much) about what I'm working on. I teach and write through personal stories, which unfortunately means you often find yourselves the subject matter for my keynotes and books. Writing a book is a lot of work, and I mostly write in my "free" time, which means during time I should be spending with you. But you are both so patient and encouraging. The week that this book became what you hold in your hands today was during a writing retreat Janet and I spent in Bentonville, and I'll always fondly remember that week. I hope that my example inspires you, Marissa, yourself an aspiring writer. You both motivate me to be the best version of myself, and I for sure have my bags packed for you. I love you both more than words can say.

NOTES

INTRODUCTION

1. *The Office*, season 4, episode 11, "Survivor Man," written by Steve Carell, directed by Paul Feig, aired November 8, 2007, on NBC.

2. The Dunning-Kruger effect, named after a 1999 paper by social psychologists David Dunning and Justin Kruger.

3. Monica Anderson, "The State of Gig Work in 2021," Pew Research Center, December 8, 2021, https://www.pewresearch.org/internet/2021/12/08/the-state-of-gig-work-in-2021/.

THE 1ST SHIFT: BELIEVE IN YOUR IMPACT

1. We started using a system called EOS# (Entrepreneurial Operating System) to run the business. If you're interested in learning more, there are two great books that teach the key elements of EOS by its founder, Gino Wickman. They are *Traction* and *Rocket Fuel*. Wickman also has a good book on leadership called *How to Be a Great Boss*. And if you're a business owner reading this book, I can't recommend the system more highly.

2. Aaron E. Carroll, "The Placebo Effect Doesn't Apply Just to Pills," *New York Times*, October 6, 2014, https://www.nytimes.com/2014/10/07/upshot/the-placebo-effect-doesnt-apply-just-to-pills.html.

3. See Brian Reid, "The Nocebo Effect: Placebo's Evil Twin," *Washington Post*, April 29, 2002, https://www.washingtonpost.com/archive/lifestyle/wellness/2002/04/30/the-nocebo-effect-placebos-evil-twin/6945da76-fb8e-401e-a4f2-0439d36f4c6a/.

4. See Rachel Brazil, "Nocebo: The Placebo Effect's Evil Twin," *Pharmaceutical Journal*, February 12, 2021, https://pharmaceutical-journal.com/article/feature/nocebo-the-placebo-effects-evil-twin#fn_5.

5. Adapted from the article "VOODOO Death," Walter Bradford Cannon, MA, MD, *American Journal of Public Health* 92, no. 10 (October 2002): 1593–1596, https://www.ncbi.nlm.nih.gov/pmc/articles/PMC1447285/ (originally published in *American Anthropologist* 44 (1942): 169–181). See also Wikipedia entry on the Mona Mona Mission (https://en.wikipedia.org/wiki/Mona_Mona_Mission).

6. Douglas McGregor and Joel E. Cutcher-Gershenfeld, *The Human Side of Enterprise*, Annotated Edition (New York: McGraw-Hill Professional, 2008).

7. There are two great books on habit formation and habit change that I highly recommend. *Atomic Habits*, by James Clear, is an outstanding book on habit change. It builds on the work of Charles Duhigg, who wrote *The Power of Habit*, which I also recommend.

THE 2ND SHIFT: BELIEVE IN YOURSELF

1. There's a funny George Carlin video that makes this point: https://www.youtube.com/watch?v=XWPCE2tTLZQ.

2. To learn more about the social psychology of cognitive biases, check out the following links. Actor–Observer Asymmetry: https://en.wikipedia.org/wiki/Actor–observer_asymmetry - bias; Fundamental Attribution Error: https://en.wikipedia.org/wiki/Fundamental_attribution_error; List of cognitive biases: https://en.wikipedia.org/wiki/List_of_cognitive_biases#Social_biases.

3. Daniel Kahneman, *Thinking, Fast and Slow* (New York: Farrar, Straus, and Giroux, 2011).

4. Mahzarin R. Banaji and Anthony G. Greenwald, *Blindspot: Hidden Biases of Good People* (New York: Delacorte Press, 2015).

5. Banaji and Greenwald, *Blindspot*.

6. Implicit Association Test: https://implicit.harvard.edu/implicit/.

7. Confirmation Bias: https://en.wikipedia.org/wiki/Confirmation_bias.

8. Noah Smith, "Authoritarians Flop as Economic Modernizers," *Bloomberg*, June 7, 2017, https://www.bloomberg.com/view/articles/2017-06-07/authoritarians-flop-as-economic-modernizers#xj4y7vzkg.

9. Cognitive Dissonance: https://en.wikipedia.org/wiki/Cognitive_dissonance.

10. See Alex Shashkevich, "Is the Placebo Effect More Powerful Than We Think?," Greater Good, March 16, 2017, https://greatergood.berkeley.edu/article/item/is_the_placebo_effect_more_powerful_than_we_think.

THE 3RD SHIFT: BELIEVE IN OTHERS

1. Joseph Campbell, *The Hero with a Thousand Faces* (Los Angeles, CA: Joseph Campbell Foundation, 2020).

2. Check out this link to watch Daniel's TED Talk: https://www.ted.com/talks /daniel_kish_how_i_use_sonar_to_navigate_the_world.

3. Daniel Kish, "#ZeroCon18—Daniel Kish | Keynote [CC]," Zero Project, Youtube, March 20, 2018, 3:30, https://www.youtube.com/ watch?v=QDB8bMu4yCM.

4. Robert Rosenthal and Kermit L. Fode, "The Effect of Experimenter Bias on the Performance of the Albino Rat," *Behavioral Science*, 8, no. 3 (1963): 183–89, https://doi.org/10.1002/bs.3830080302.

5. Robert Rosenthal and Lenore Jacobson, *Pygmalion in the Classroom: Teacher Expectation and Pupils' Intellectual Development* (Carmarthen: Crown House, 1992).

6. See Ian J. Deary et al., "The Stability of Individual Differences in Mental Ability from Childhood to Old Age: Follow-Up of the 1932 Scottish Mental Survey," *Intelligence* 28, no. 1 (February 2000): 49–55, https://www.sciencedirect.com /science/article/pii/S0160289699000318. Children's IQs can go up, especially if this is the first time they've attended school, and the Rosenthal and Jacobson study was done on first and second graders. However, their results were far outside expected changes for first-time elementary students.

THE 4TH SHIFT: BELIEVE IN YOUR RELATIONSHIPS

1. Kim and Tom aren't their real names.

2. Charles Duhigg, "What Google Learned from Its Quest to Build the Perfect Team," *New York Times*, February 25, 2016, https://www.nytimes.com/2016/02 /28/magazine/what-google-learned-from-its-quest-to-build-the-perfect-team .html?_r=0.

3. Amy Edmondson, "Psychological Safety and Learning Behavior in Work Teams," *Administrative Science Quarterly* 44, no. 2 (June 1999): 350–383, https://doi.org /10.2307/2666999.

4. Duhigg, "What Google Learned from Its Quest to Build a Perfect Team."

5. I first mentioned these questions in a blog post I wrote in 2017, which was based on an article I read somewhere. I've never been able to find the original source. If you happen to have seen these before, could you let me know? I'd like to link to them and thank the author for the inspiration.

6. Edgar H. Schein and Peter A. Schein, *Humble Inquiry: The Gentle Art of Asking instead of Telling* (San Francisco, CA: Berrett-Koehler Publishers, Inc., 2013).

7. See Benjamin Franklin, *The Autobiography of Benjamin Franklin* (New York: Simon & Schuster, 2004). I first read this story in Adam Grant's terrific book *Give and Take*, where he is quoting Ben Franklin's biographer Walter Isaacson (a biography I also highly recommend).

8. Daniel Coyle, *The Culture Playbook: 60 Highly Effective Actions to Help Your Group Succeed* (New York: Bantam Publishers, Inc., 2022).

9. The 5-5-5 quarterly discussion approach is part of the Entrepreneurial Operating System process, which I've modified somewhat (their version doesn't ask the employee to give feedback to the leader, which I think is important). I'm summarizing it here, and I encourage any leader interested in learning more to check out *Traction* by Gino Wickman. If you are a company owner reading this, I highly recommend checking out EOS.

10. Gallup, "Indicator: Employee Engagement," Gallup.com, July 20, 2023, https ://www.gallup.com/394373/indicator-employee-engagement.aspx.

11. Jon Clifton, "Why the World Can't Quit Quiet Quitting," Gallup.com, June 21, 2023, https://www.gallup.com/workplace/507650/why-world-quit-quiet -quitting.aspx.

12. Jim Harter, "Is Quiet Quitting Real?," Gallup.com, September 6, 2023, https ://www.gallup.com/workplace/398306/quiet-quitting-real.aspx.

13. Timothy M. Gardner, Chad H. Van Iddekinge, and Peter W. Hom, "If You've Got Leavin' on Your Mind: The Identification and Validation of Pre-Quitting Behaviors," *Journal of Management* 44, no. 8 (2016): 3231–57, https://doi.org /10.1177/0149206316665462.

14. Gino Wickman, *Traction: Get a Grip on Your Business* (Dallas, TX: BenBella Books, 2012).

15. See Mandy Len Catron, "To Fall in Love with Anyone, Do This," *New York Times*, January 11, 2015, https://www.nytimes.com/2015/01/11/style/modern -love-to-fall-in-love-with-anyone-do-this.html.

16. Arthur Aron et al., "The Experimental Generation of Interpersonal Closeness: A Procedure and Some Preliminary Findings," *Personality and Social Psychology Bulletin* 23, no. 4 (April 1997): 363–377, https://journals.sagepub.com/doi/ pdf/10.1177/0146167297234003.

17. See https://www.businessballs.com/self-awareness/johari-window-model-and -free-diagrams/.

MAKE IT HAPPEN

1. The best book on building a team I've ever read is *The Five Dysfunctions of a Team* by Patrick Lencioni. It's a classic for a reason. We have used this as the framework for all our team building at my company over the past four years. If you've avoided it for years like I did, do yourself a favor and read it (right after you finish this book ☺)

2. You can find our complete list of core values at https://lrionline.com/about-lri/.

3. The Three Questions of Approachable Leaders are: Do you have what you need? What would make work better? What's next? Check out *The Approachability Playbook* and our Approachable Leadership Workshop to learn more about the Three Questions and how to use them in your day-to-day leadership at approachableleadership.com.

4. Here I am outlining coaching discussions without reference to the specific policies that are in place in your company. Don't take or recommend any employment action unless and until you document and follow your company's policies. Consult your human resources expert before taking any disciplinary action, and often these situations also require legal advice.

CONCLUSION

1. Cameron G. Brown, "Leader Approachability: What Is It, What Is It Good for, and Who Needs It?" The University of Tulsa ProQuest Dissertations Publishing, Accession No. 10146605 (2016), https://www.proquest.com/openview/8e6d69 5e6283293a56bdd70eaf5c7e66/1.

2. Josh Royes and Phillip B. Wilson, "Leader Approachability: Reduced Turnover and Other Business Outcomes," *Approachable Leadership*, accessed June 8, 2023, https://approachableleadership.com/wp-content/uploads/2021/05/Leader -Approachability-Reduced-Turnover-and-Other-Business-Outcomes.pdf.

3. Brown, "Leader Approachability."

4. This section is based on Martin E. P. Seligman's terrific book *Learned Optimism: How to Change Your Mind and Your Life* (London: Nicholas Brealey, 2018). See also Martin Seligman and Peter Schulman, "Explanatory Style as a Predictor of Productivity and Quitting among Life Insurance Sales Agents," *Journal of Personality and Social Psychology* 50, no. 4 (1986): 832–838, https:// doi.org/10.1037/0022-3514.50.4.832.

5. Michelle Gielan, "The Financial Upside of Being an Optimist," *Harvard Business Review*, March 12, 2019, https://hbr.org/2019/03/the-financial-upside-of-being-an-optimist.

6. Ron Kaniel, Cade Massey, and David T. Robinson, "The Importance of Being an Optimist: Evidence from Labor Markets," National Bureau of Economic Research, September 2, 2010, http://www.nber.org/papers/w16328.

7. Jack Zenger and Joseph Folkman, "If Your Boss Thinks You're Awesome, You Will Become More Awesome," *Harvard Business Review*, January 27, 2015, https://hbr.org/2015/01/if-your-boss-thinks-youre-awesome-you-will-become-more-awesome.

8. See H. Song et al., "Improving Relationships by Elevating Positive Illusion and the Underlying Psychological and Neural Mechanisms," *Frontiers in Human Neuroscience* 12, no. 526 (January 11, 2019): https://doi.org/10.3389/fnhum.2018.00526. See also Sandra Murray, John Holmes, and Dale Griffin, "The Self-Fulfilling Nature of Positive Illusions in Romantic Relationships: Love Is Not Blind, but Prescient," *Journal of Personality and Social Psychology* 71, no. 6 (December 1996): 1155–1180, https://doi.org/10.1037/0022-3514.71.6.1155.

9. Danu Stinson, Jessica Cameron, Joanne Wood, Danielle Gaucher, and John Holmes, "Deconstructing the 'Reign of Error': Interpersonal Warmth Explains the Self-Fulfilling Prophecy of Anticipated Acceptance," *Personality and Social Psychology Bulletin* 35, no. 9 (July 1, 2009): 1165-1178, https://doi.org/10.1177/0146167209338629.

10. Hayami K. Koga et al., "Optimism, Lifestyle, and Longevity in a Racially Diverse Cohort of Women," *Journal of the American Geriatrics Society* 70, no. 10 (June 8, 2022): 2793-2804, https://doi.org/10.1111/jgs.17897.

11. Lewina O. Lee, Peter James, and Emily S. Zevon, "Optimism Is Associated with Exceptional Longevity in 2 Epidemiologic Cohorts of Men and Women," *PNAS* 116, no. 37 (August 26, 2019): 18357–18362, https://doi.org/10.1073/pnas.1900712116.

12. Stacey L. Hart, Lea Vella, and David C. Mohr, "Relationships among Depressive Symptoms, Benefit-Finding, Optimism, and Positive Affect in Multiple Sclerosis Patients after Psychotherapy for Depression," *Health Psychology* 27, no. 2 (2008): 230–238, https://doi.org/10.1037/0278-6133.27.2.230.

13. Jameson K. Hirsch, Kenneth R. Conner, and Paul R. Duberstein, "Optimism and Suicide Ideation among Young Adult College Students," *Archives of Suicide Research* 11, no. 2 (2007): 177–185, https://doi.org/10.1080/13811110701249988.

14. Becca R. Levy, Martin D. Slade, Suzanne R. Kunkel, and Stanislav V. Kasl, "Longevity Increased by Positive Self-Perceptions of Aging," *American Psychological Association* 83, no. 2 (August 2002): 261–270, https://doi.org/10.1037/0022-3514.83.2.261.

15. Becca R. Levy et al., "Reducing Cardiovascular Stress with Positive Self-Stereotypes of Aging," *The Journals of Gerontology: Series B* 55, no. 4 (July 1, 2000): P205–P213, https://doi.org/10.1093/geronb/55.4.P205.

ABOUT THE AUTHOR

 **PHILLIP B. WILSON** is the founder of Approachable Leadership, where he and his team help clients thrive and create extraordinary workplaces. He is a national expert on leadership, labor relations, and creating positive workplaces. He is regularly featured in the business media, including *Fox Business News*, *Fast Company*, *Bloomberg News*, *HR Magazine*, and *The New York Times*.

Wilson is a highly regarded author, speaker, and trainer. Phil delivers keynotes, workshops, and webinars regularly for conferences, industry groups, and companies across North America and Canada.

Phil is the author of multiple books and publications. In addition to *The Leader-Shift Playbook*, he authored *The Approachability Playbook* and *Left of Boom: Putting Proactive Engagement to Work* (which reached #2 on Amazon's Hot HR Books list). Other books and publications include: *The Next 52 Weeks*, *Managing the Union Shop*, and *Model Contract Clauses*, among many others.

Phil has been called on multiple occasions to testify before Congress as a labor relations expert. He graduated magna cum laude from Augustana College in Rock Island, Illinois, and went on to earn his J.D. from the University of Michigan Law School.

CREATING YOUR LEADER-SHIFT
Become an Approachable Leader and Create an Extraordinary Workplace

A t **Approachable Leadership** we are dedicated to helping our clients create extraordinary workplaces (#EXWP). We do this by training leaders to harness the power of approachability, the 4 Leader-Shifts, and how to shrink power distance. We help clients of every size and in every industry, from the Fortune 50 to small entrepreneurial and community organizations.

TO LEARN MORE ABOUT MAKING YOUR WORKPLACE EXTRAORDINARY, VISIT YOURLEADERSHIFT.COM OR CALL 800-888-9115.

Here are a few of the useful resources we offer to clients.

Keynote Presentations: Looking for a keynote that will move and inspire your audience to become better leaders? Our keynote presentations on Approachable Leadership and *The Leader-Shift Playbook* are fully customizable for your audience and event. We've presented to audiences of all sizes and in every type of organization. Our consistently high-rated talks blend humor, emotion, and the latest research with practical takeaways. Your leaders leave excited about being better leaders at work and at home.

The Approachable Leadership° Learning System: An immersive, interactive series of half-day experiences. Designed for cohorts of up to 25 leaders who learn and practice core approachability skills. Each workshop builds on prior experiences and every learner leaves each workshop with a 60-day plan to implement what they learn.

Approachable Leadership Consulting: We help clients measure the approachability of their leaders, identify gaps, and offer guidance on steps you can take to transform your organization into an EXWP (extraordinary workplace). In addition to our Learning System, we can individually coach leaders and provide organizational design advice to increase leader approachability in your company.

Help Spread the Word about
THE LEADER-SHIFT PLAYBOOK
and Approachable Leadership

Help us spread the word about *The Leader-Shift Playbook* and Approachable Leadership! Here are four things you can do now:

1. **Share the Book:** Know someone who would enjoy *The Leader-Shift Playbook*? All you have to do is go to YourLeaderShift. com and click on "Share the Book." We will send an excerpt and a discount code (with your compliments). What's more approachable than that?

2. **Join the Conversation:** Connect with me on LinkedIn (LinkedIn. com/in/pbwilson) and let your network know about *The Leader-Shift Playbook,* your approachability journey, and how you're creating an EXWP (extraordinary workplace). Use the hashtags #TheLeaderShift, #EXWP, #HeroAssumption, and #ApproachableLeadership so we can find your post and say thanks! Anything you can do to spread the word is greatly appreciated.

3. **Bring Approachable Leadership° to Your Company or Community:** Whether you need a keynote speaker for your next company training, industry or professional association event, or want to deliver our Learning System to your leaders, we'd love to discuss the options. We customize our message for any group. Learn more by clicking "Speaking" at YourLeaderShift.com.

4. **Share Your Experience:** Tell us what you think! A short review on the retailer site of your choosing is so helpful in spreading the word. And we love hearing directly from readers about how they've applied our teaching in their lives. Let us know how it's helped you, if you have questions, or if there is anything we can do to make this material more useful to you or your team. Experiencing challenges or roadblocks? Let us know. We'll coach you through it. Just click on "Contact" at YourLeaderShift.com.